Geopolitical Dynamism of India-Tajikistan Relations

Geopolitical Dynamism of India-Tajikistan Relations

Edited by

Jyotsna Bakshi

INDIAN COUNCIL OF WORLD AFFAIRS

PENTAGON PRESS

Geopolitical Dynamism of India-Tajikistan Relations
Editor: Jyotsna Bakshi

ISBN 978-81-8274-728-9

First Published in 2013

The responsibility for facts and opinions in this publication rests exclusively with the authors and their interpretations do not necessarily reflect the views or the policy of the Indian Council of World Affairs, New Delhi.

Published by

PENTAGON PRESS
206, Peacock Lane, Shahpur Jat,
New Delhi-110049
Phones: 011-64706243, 26491568
Telefax: 011-26490600
email: rajan@pentagonpress.in
website: www.pentagonpress.in

Printed at Avantika Printers Private Limited.

Contents

Foreword

Sudhir Devare, DG, ICWA (April 2009-April 2012)

India's contact with Central Asia goes back to the ancient Silk Route days. Central Asia, connecting Asia with Europe was the hub for cultural and commercial exchanges in ancient days. The Kushan period and the Mughal Empire in India are further testimony of our deep rooted historical and cultural ties. The 19th century was marked by the rivalry between Russian and British empires over Central Asia. The Anglo-Russian Convention of 1907 ended the rivalry between the two empires, clearly demarcating their areas of influence. As a result of understanding between the two powers, Central Asia came under Russian control. This also ended India's interaction with the region.

However, after India's Independence, our good relations with the former Soviet Union paved the way for India's contact with Soviet Central Asia. India was one of the few countries that had contacts with the region during the Soviet period, which was influenced from Moscow. The birth of five independent Central Asian Republics (CARs) in 1991, following their independence opened doors for direct interaction. Strategic location and rich natural resources have attracted tremendous international attention to the region after the disintegration of the Soviet Union, which also intensified competition among various players jockeying to gain a foothold in the region.

India enjoys a growing and friendly relationship with the Central

Asian countries. The five republics also see India as a friendly nation, which makes India a more preferable partner for the republics. However, our historical ties with the region perhaps did not fully reflect in our engagement with the region in post Soviet days. Of late, India's initiatives with the region demonstrate our renewed interest in cultivating stronger ties with the CARs. One of the important milestones in our engagement with Central Asia has been the visit by the Kazakh President Nursultan Nazarbayev to India as the chief guest at the 2009 Republic Day function. This was the first time India invited a Central Asian President to grace the occasion. A few important visits in the past few years speak of the mutual interests in deepening ties. Some of the notable high-level visits that took place in the last four years are—Vice President Hamid Ansari's visit to Turkmenistan and Kazakhstan in 2008, President Pratibha Devisingh Patil's visit to Tajikistan in 2009, Turkmen President Gurbanguly Berdimuhamedov's visit to India in 2010, Prime Minister Manmohan Singh's visit to Kazakhstan in 2011 and Uzbek President Islam Karimov's visit to India in May 2011.

India has been cultivating bilateral ties with the five republics. Understanding the individual needs of these republics is in India's interest in the region. Among the five CARs, Tajikistan has its own significance in the region. The Republic is nearest to India and shares the longest border with Afghanistan in the region, which makes Tajikistan strategically important for India. It is, therefore, essential to understand the dynamics of India-Tajikistan ties.

The three day visit by Indian President to Tajikistan from September 6-8, 2009 was a landmark development in our bilateral relations. She is the first Indian President to visit Tajikistan and the first foreigner to participate in the national day celebration of Tajikistan. The prime purpose of the visit was to enhance 'goodwill, trust and mutual confidence' between the two countries.

The deteriorating situation in Afghanistan and the security challenges that both face from this, features prominently in our bilateral talks. Stability in Afghanistan is a desired goal for both, bringing the two countries closer. The U.S. decision to pull out its troops from

Afghan soil by 2014 has added to the uncertainties in the country, calling for greater cooperation among the regional countries. The long porous Tajik-Afghan border makes Tajikistan vulnerable to extremism, drug trafficking and refugees emanating from Afghanistan. The resurgence of the Taliban, the growing influence of extremist forces and drug trafficking are worrying both India and Tajikistan.

During President Patil's visit to the Republic two years ago 'terrorism emanating from Afghanistan' found special mention in bilateral discussions. Sharing similar security concerns, both India and Tajikistan are cooperating to fight terrorism in the region.

Significantly, India and Tajikistan decided to raise their bilateral ties to the level of strategic partnership during the visit of Tajik President Emomali Rahmon to New Delhi from September 1-4, 2012.

Giving a push to India's 'Connect Central Asia Policy', External Affairs Minister, S.M. Krishna visited the Tajik capital in July 2012. In Dushanbe, the External Affairs Minister also addressed a conference of Indian ambassadors in the Eurasian region.

Tajikistan is taking keen interest in playing an active role in regional issues, which has enhanced its geo-political status in the region. On 30 July 2009, Tajikistan hosted the quadripartite meeting at Dushanbe for the first time, which included Tajikistan, Pakistan, Afghanistan and Russia. This quadripartite group met again in 2010 at Sochi and at Dushanbe in 2011. Tajikistan is also part of the Central Asia-South Asia Electricity Transmission and Trade Project (CASA 1000), a project aimed at transmitting electricity from Central Asia to South Asia. It will enable Tajikistan to export 1,000 MW of electricity to Pakistan and Afghanistan. India is excluded from both these regional initiatives. Strengthening India-Tajikistan bilateral ties could in future pave the way for India's involvement in these regional projects.

Tajikistan has the richest water resources in the region and it is the second largest producer of hydroelectricity. Cooperation in the hydroelectric sector is one promising area of enhancing economic cooperation. India is already engaged in the Tajik hydropower sector. Two Indian companies, BHEL and NHPC are modernising the Varzob-1 hydro power station. It is worth exploring the possibility of

India buying electricity from Tajikistan. The country is also rich in mineral resources like aluminium, gold, silver, uranium, etc.

One weak area in our relationship with the region in general is the low trade turn over. India's trade with Tajikistan is extremely low. Lack of connectivity is one major impediment in developing stronger trade ties between the two countries as well as with the other republics. Indian investments in Tajikistan, one of the poorest economies in the region could help the Republic to revitalise its economy. It would also facilitate to deepen India's economic presence in the country. Tourism, pharmaceuticals, health, education, science and technology, communication and agricultural goods processing industry are a few areas that have already been identified as areas where Indian investments are welcome. Both sides have also started a weekly Dushanbe-Delhi direct flight since February 2011.

Another possible area of our engagement with the CARs could be defence cooperation, which remains low at present. It is an area worth exploring. Among the five republics, our defence cooperation with Tajikistan has been relatively active. India renovated and upgraded the Ayni airport, situated close to Dushanbe. India is providing military training to Tajik military personnel in Indian institutes. Tajikistan is the only country in the region to have a formal Defence Agreement with India.

Tajikistan, like the other CARs is witnessing competition among various players. India's relationship with Tajikistan as well as with the other republics has to take into account the presence and influence of various powers involved in the region. Multi-vectored foreign policy practiced by the five republics has helped India find place in the geo-political space of the region. Do the CARs see India as a balancer or stabiliser in the region?

The Shanghai Cooperation Organisation (SCO) is an important multi-lateral group in the region, which is gradually evolving. Established as Shanghai 5 in 1996, it became the Shanghai Cooperation Organisation with Uzbekistan joining the group in 2001. The present members include Russia, China, Kazakhstan, Uzbekistan, Kyrgyzstan and Tajikistan. India joined the Organisation as an observer in 2005.

Other observer member countries are Mongolia, Pakistan and Iran. In addition to our bilateral engagements, full membership in SCO would be another means to upgrade India's relationship with the five republics. India is not a member of any regional groups in Central Asia. Membership in SCO would give India a common platform to discuss regional issues with the CARs and the two influential regional powers-Russia and China. India, of late has shown willingness to become a full member of the Organisation. India's recent interest in SCO membership also reflects our renewed interest in revitalising ties with the region. India's membership has found support from Tajikistan and also from the other member Central Asian countries.

The present edited volume, which puts together the papers presented at the conference held between the Tajik Academy of Sciences (TAS) and the Indian Council of World Affairs (ICWA) in June 2010, has broadly covered the entire gamut of India-Tajikistan relations. The book is an interesting study analysing our engagement beginning from the ancient period to contemporary times. The book also throws light on our deep-rooted historical and cultural ties, especially the role played by literature in connecting people from both these countries. Translations done by Tajik scholars of Indian classics and vice-versa have opened doors to mutual knowledge of our societies. In-depth discussion on wide range of contemporary issues like India's role in the region, convergence of interests between India and Tajikistan, the Afghanistan factor and various other aspects of our bilateral relationship have added to the contemporary relevance of the study, providing an understanding of how to further enhance the scope for our bilateral engagements. I trust this volume will help promote better communication and understanding between India and Tajikistan.

Contributors

Abdunabi Sattorzoda, Head of Political Department, Centre for Strategic Studies under the Office of the President of Tajikistan.

G.M. Maytdinova, Professor of History and International Relations Theory and Director of the Centre for Geopolitical Studies at the Russian-Tajik Slavonic University, Dushanbe, Republic of Tajikistan.

Habibullo Rajabob is the Head of the Department of Indian Philology at the Tajik National University, Republic of Tajikistan.

Jyotsna Bakshi has lived and worked in Central Asia as India Chair Professor in the University of World Economy and Diplomacy, Tashkent from 2006 to 2009 and as Associate Professor in the Centre for Indian Studies at Osh State University, Kyrgyzstan from 2002 to 2005.

Khaibatullo Shodiev, Prominent scholar from the Republic of Tajikistan.

Mahmadshoh I. Ilolov, President of the Academy of Sciences of the Republic of Tajikistan.

Meena Singh Roy, Research Fellow at the Institute for Defence Studies and Analyses, New Delhi, India.

Mirzo Mulloahmedov, Prominent scholar from the Republic of Tajikistan.

Muzaffar Olimov, Director of Research Centre 'Sharq', Dushanbe, Republic of Tajikistan.

Rajiv Dogra had a distinguished career as a member of Indian Foreign Service. He served as Indian Ambassador to various countries.

Saodat Olimova, Head of Sociological Research in Research Centre, '*Sharq*', Dushanbe, Republic of Tajikistan.

Sh. Sufiev, Institute of Oriental Studies and Written Heritage at the Tajik Academy of Sciences, Republic of Tajikistan.

Sudhir Devare, Director General, Indian Council of World Affairs (April 2009 to April 2012), New Delhi, India.

Victor Dubovitsky, Doctor of Historical Sciences, Deputy Director of the Institute of History, Archeology and Ethnography of the Tajik Academy of Sciences, Republic of Tajikistan.

Introduction

Jyotsna Bakshi

The present volume is a collection of papers presented at the first India-Tajikistan joint conference held in Dushanbe on June 29, 2010. The conference was organised by the Indian Council of World Affairs (ICWA) and the Tajik Academy of Sciences. These two premier academic institutions of India and Tajikistan had in 2006 signed a Memorandum of Understanding (MoU) regarding mutual cooperation.

The geopolitical dynamism of India-Tajikistan relations is determined by consciousness of deep-rooted historical and cultural ties, shared values and beliefs, similar threat perceptions and identity of interests in fostering peaceful and stable common neighbourhood. One common strand running through all the papers is a profound awareness of and indeed reverence for the deep-rooted historical and cultural ties between the two countries. Over the centuries, a dense cultural and ethnic intermingling has taken place between the peoples of the Indian Subcontinent and Central Asia leading to mutual enrichment and deep-rooted sense of mutual trust and understanding. This spirit of mutual trust and appreciation imbues every aspect of India-Tajikistan bilateral relations. Besides broad compatibility of their geopolitical interests, India and Tajikistan have also shared through the millennia a common geo-cultural space. Bonds of culture and history have further helped the two governments and peoples to seek common moorings in rather fluid and uncertain geopolitical dynamics of contemporary regional and world politics. The two countries share a common belief in the values of pluralism, secularism and tolerance.

Speeches by Director General ICWA Mr. Sudhir Devare and the President of the Tajik Academy of Sciences, Academician Mahmadshoh Ilolov as the heads of the Indian and Tajik delegations at the conference set the tone of the present discourse by touching on major issues. The stress was on looking forward and building on common concerns and interests. Academician Ilolov's 'Opening Remarks at the Conference' are included in this volume.

As members of the Indian delegation, Ambassador Rajiv Dogra (former Joint Secretary Eurasia in the Indian Ministry of External Affairs), then Indian Ambassador in Dushanbe Mr. Amar Sinha, then Deputy Director General, ICWA, Dr. Ramesh Chandra made a weighty contribution to the conference by bringing in their rich experience and knowledge of working in or with this region. Dr. Jyotsna Bakshi, who had earlier served as India Chair Professor in the universities in Kyrgyzstan and Uzbekistan and Dr. Meena Singh Roy of the Institute of Defence Studies and Analysis, New Delhi, represented academic institutions at the conference.

This volume includes three papers by the Indian side and eight papers by the Tajik side. The papers by the Tajik scholars were originally written and presented in Russian language. The Indian Embassy in Tajikistan has done a commendable job in making their English translations available. Thus, the present volume provides an opportunity to Tajik scholars to make their views and perspectives known to a wider readership in India as well as the non-Russian-speaking world at large.

The uncertainties surrounding the troubled 'Af-Pak' region, especially compounded by the US decision to start a phased withdrawal of the bulk of troops from Afghanistan between July 2011-2014, make it imperative for neighbouring countries like India and the Central Asian states, including Tajikistan, to enter into mutual consultations to search for ways to maintain peace and stability in the region. Indeed, a couple of papers in this volume by the Tajik scholars explicitly call for Indian initiative to maintain balance and stability in the region. Abdunabi Sattorzoda of the Institute of Strategic Studies under the President of Tajikistan doubts the efficacy of recent U.S. policy to reach some agreement with the Taliban. According to him what Afghanistan needs is the formation of a government of 'national unity' which may satisfy the aspirations of its diverse ethnic groups. He thinks that India and Tajikistan must work together to bring the various actors from all ethnic groups in Afghanistan closer to each other. Otherwise, Afghanistan will continue to remain at war. He also believes that India and Tajikistan can join hands in trying to bring closer the positions of various powers involved in Afghanistan in the interest of peace in the region.

Victor Dubovitsky is of the opinion that India can consolidate all the 'constructive forces' in the southern sub-region of Eurasia in the struggle against political and religious extremism. In his view "India possesses both resources and political will for this purpose."

Tajik scholars and analysts like Sattorzoda, Dubovitsky and Maytdinova expect India to play a stabilising role in the current complex geopolitical scenario in the region. Maytdinova has suggested a 'seven plus five' formula for Afghan settlement with the participation of seven neighbouring countries, viz., India, Pakistan, Iran, China, Tajikistan, Uzbekistan and Turkmenistan along with five other important players namely, USA, Russia, NATO, CSTO and SCO. She suggests a neutral status for Afghanistan.

In their paper 'Tajik-Indian Relations in the Mirror of Public Opinion in Tajikistan,' Saodat Alimova and Muzaffar Alimov have found on the basis of their research survey that the majority of Tajik people regard India as a friendly and non-threatening country.

In the backdrop of a broad panoramic view of millennia old cultural and economic interactions between the peoples of India and Central Asia, Ambassador Rajiv Dogra has pointedly drawn attention to the curtailing of these ties during the British rule in India. He raises the question whether it was a matter of deliberate policy or coincidence. He analyses the factors that have hindered a more robust cooperation between India and Tajikistan in recent times and points towards the way forward by enlisting the key areas in which the two sides can cooperate despite turbulent and none too helpful situation in the common neighbourhood.

Jyotsna Bakshi's paper deals with common concerns and shared interests of India and Tajikistan in the evolving regional geopolitics. The two countries have a vital stake in peace and stability in their common neighbourhood for their accelerated economic development. According to her the best case scenario would be cooperation among all the major powers and regional players for establishing peace in Afghanistan and promoting shared prosperity through improved transport connectivity, enhanced trade and greater people-to-people contacts.

Meena Singh Roy's comprehensive paper deals with various facets of India-Tajikistan bilateral ties. She has presented a comparative analysis of the share of Central Asian states in India's overall trade. With the help of tables and figures she has provided valuable data on India's economic and security engagement with all the Central Asian states with special reference to Tajikistan.

As has already been mentioned, cultural and literary interactions form an inalienable part of India-Tajikistan relations. This volume contains three papers by eminent Tajik experts on this aspect. Habibullo Rajabov has beautifully traced how translations of literary masterpieces in each other's languages have brought the people of the two countries together.

Tajik language is a branch of Persian. In the rich and diverse culture of India, Persian language and literature have a special role. During the medieval era, Persian was the court language in India. As Sh. Sufiev has pointed out, during this period more literary works were produced in India in Persian language than in all other Persian-speaking areas. This period of Indian history is called 'the Indian summer of the Persian literature.' Mulloahmedov's paper deals with Tajik-Iranian relations and finds a common Indian connection. Tajik scholars and researchers have a great interest in the vast treasure house of old Persian manuscripts available in India.

It is hoped that the present volume may make its own small

contribution in fostering India-Tajikistan multi-faceted relations, which is in the interest of both countries.

It may be clarified that the views expressed here are individual opinions of the authors and not of the institution sponsoring the publication of this volume.

As editor of this volume I have great pleasure in expressing sincere thanks to Director General ICWA Mr. Sudhir Devare. Without his constant interest and support, the publication of this volume would not have been possible. Our sincere thanks also go to the President of the Tajik Academy of Sciences, Academician Mahmadshoh Ilolov. He and his colleagues did everything to make the joint Indian-Tajik academic meet a brilliant success. Ambassador Amar Sinha and other members of the Indian Embassy in Dushanbe worked with great enthusiasm and acumen to make the Indiandelegation's visit extremely fruitful and pleasant. I am also thankful to the then DDG of ICWA, Dr. Ramesh Chandra. Dr. Angira Sen Sarma, a Research Fellow at the ICWA, has contributed by coordinating the publication of this volume. Last but not the least, my special thanks are due to all the contributors to this volume.

Opening Remarks by the President of Academy of Sciences of the Republic of Tajikistan

Mahmadshoh I. Ilolov

Historical and cultural ties between the Indian and Tajik people have a long history. Common Aryan roots of the sedentary people populating the Hindustani peninsula and the territory of the ancient Maverannahr[1] and Khorasan[2] became the primary basis of continuity of these relations. Tracing the history of relations between numerous states that existed in the territory of these regions, we can confidently assert that they always shared continuous and multifarious political, economic and cultural contacts. These ties mutually enrich our peoples by adding new elements and colour to their lives.

Owing to close and deep intermingling of peoples inhabiting the two regions, who can say today which specific Indian motives were borrowed in the work of Borbad, the great Tajik composer of the ninth/tenth centuries or who can assess the exact contribution of Indian architects in the construction of stone masterpieces of Samarkand in the 15th century? Tajikistan and India are inextricably linked by names like Abu Ali ibn Sina (Avicenna), Rozi Zakaria[3] and dozens of other scientists and scholars who worked in Central Asia as well as in India. At present India has the Academy of Avicenna, and in Mumbai, there are over a hundred centres of traditional Ayurvedic medicine, that work on the 'Canon of Medical Science' of our great compatriot, Avicenna.

Outstanding Tajik scientists and scholars—Babajan Ghafurov and Muhammad Asimov—made a great contribution to the development of academic and scientific relations between our two countries. They are the authors of dozens of monographs and scientific articles on the people of India, its politics and culture. Academician M. Asimov was the initiator of the two Indo-Tajik scientific symposia held in Mumbai in 1980 and 1982.

Of course, in different epochs the contacts between our peoples acquired new forms and also varied in intensity. Often they were reflected in the relations among other powers in the region. Thus, during the 19th century, Britain and Russia emerged as the main contenders in the struggle for influence in the region of the Middle East. This grandiose geopolitical battle between the two superpowers is known in history as 'Great Game'. Here we must recall that the central object of the geopolitical struggle of the 'British Lion' and 'Russian bear' became India – 'the biggest jewel in the crown of the British Empire.' The 'Great Game' of geopolitical rivals had been guided—at times without real facts—by political myths created for internal use or external propaganda about India. For more than a century there raged diplomatic passions, intense struggle of intelligence services and big and small wars broke out. In this tussle, a key 'battleground' was the territory of Central Asia, including Tajikistan.

Those days are now over and the Republic of Tajikistan and the Republic of India are developing their relations as sovereign states.

Diplomatic relations of the Republic of India and the Republic of Tajikistan were established in 1993. However, on actual enhancing of bilateral relations between the two countries, it was in 1995 that the official visit of the President of the Republic of Tajikistan, H.E. Emomali Sharipovich Rahmon, to New Delhi took place. During the visit, a number of fundamental documents were signed, including the Declaration on further development and deepening of friendly relations between the Republic of Tajikistan and the Republic of India and the agreement on commerce and investment protection.

In 1996 the Ministry of Foreign Affairs of Tajikistan stated that:

> "In the political field the positions of the Republic of India on a number of regional and international issues are identical with or are very similar to the positions of the Republic of Tajikistan."

In 1996 India provided a loan of $ 5 million to Tajikistan. This was a significant aid to our country under difficult conditions of the civil war. In August of the same year, the Government of Tajikistan took the decision of opening its trade mission in India.

In 1997 there was some intensification of cooperation in cultural and educational spheres. This was promoted by the implementation of an agreement between the two countries regarding the Cultural Exchange Programme for 1996 and 1998. Within the framework of this programme, prominent scientists and the representatives of the education system of India visited Tajikistan. Since that time, specialists from our country are regularly getting language and diplomatic training in India.

A new impetus to bilateral Tajik-Indian relations was given by the official visit of President E.S. Rahmon to the Republic of India from May 9 to 11, 2001. During the visit, meetings and negotiations were held between the two heads of state, as well as between the Tajik President and the Prime Minister and Chairman of the Upper House of Parliament of India. The visit concluded with the signing of solid legal instruments, such as: the Joint Declaration between the Republic of Tajikistan and the Republic of India on the Principles of Mutual Relations; the Agreement between the Republic of Tajikistan and the Republic of India on the Legal Relations in Criminal Cases; the Agreement between the Government of Tajikistan and the Republic of India on Cooperation in Combating Illegal Drug Trafficking, psychotropic substances and precursors; the agreement between the Government of the Republic of Tajikistan and the Government of the Republic of India on air services and a number of other important documents.

A trend of development of relations between the two countries in security and defence field was observed in 2002. During the year visits and business contacts of parliamentarians, ministers of defence and security of the two countries took place.

At the end of 2002, New Delhi hosted the first meeting of the joint Tajik-Indian commission for trade-economic and technical cooperation, which has witnessed increased forms of cooperation in other fields, in particular the military-technical. Thus, with the help of India a full-scale modernisation of the military airfield 'Ayni' in the vicinity of Dushanbe was carried out. The airfield is currently shared by the air forces of Tajikistan and Russia—the two important geopolitical allies of India in the territory of Eurasia.

Currently, academic and scientific relations between our two countries are governed by the agreement on cooperation between Tajikistan and India, which was signed by the two Governments in 2006, during the state visit of the delegation of the Republic of Tajikistan headed by President E. Rahmon to India. As part of this contract of August 7, 2006, an agreement for cooperation in the field of science and technology was signed between the Academy of Sciences of the Republic of Tajikistan and the Department of Science and Technology of India. We are pleased to announce that at the present time within the framework of this agreement, an active scientific cooperation is taking place between Indian Biologists and Geneticists and the Institute of Plant Physiology of Academy of Sciences of Tajikistan.

Today's international conference 'The geopolitical dynamics of the Indo-Tajik relations' is also being held under the above-mentioned agreement.

The modern geopolitical situation in the world, including that in the south of Eurasia, is one of the most important elements of current world politics. The unprecedented growth of world tensions, associated with political and religious extremism, separatism and environmental issues, is forcing political scientists and experts from various countries to seek solutions of complex, at the same time old, international conflicts.

For our two countries, such a dangerous international cataclysm happens to be the conflict in Afghanistan, which for more than 30 years is threatening not only regional but also global stability. Finding ways to resolve this conflict is one of the difficult but necessary tasks for the countries bordering on Afghanistan.

Many serious problems also remain in post-Soviet space. The current situation in Kyrgyzstan is a typical example to it.

In conclusion to my welcome speech I want to wish the organisers and participants of the conference 'The Geopolitical Dynamics of the Indo-Tajik Relations' a successful and fruitful work for the benefit of science and people of Tajikistan and India!

NOTES

1. Editor's note: Maverannahr, denotes the land between two main rivers of Central Asia i.e. Syr Darya and Amu Darya, which is home to historical Central Asian cities like Samarkand Bukhara and has been the centre of Central Asian civilisation.
2. Editor's note: The term Khorasan was broadly applied for the area comprising northeastern Iran, southern Central Asia and north-western Afghanistan.
3. Editor's note: Abu Bakr Muhammad ibn Zakariya al-Razi (865- 925) was one of the famous medieval medicine practitioner and scholar. Born in Persian city of Rayy, he served in the Samanid court in Central Asia.

1

India as a Factor of Stabilisation in the Region

Abdunabi Sattorzoda

India has a special place in the foreign policy of Tajikistan given its prominent role in the region and the world, the centuries-old historical and cultural ties with Persian-speaking people, as well as its enormous economic and technological capability. India is also attractive for our country with its commitment to democracy, policy of tolerance and opposition to religious fanaticism, international terrorism and extremism.

There are a variety of areas of mutually beneficial cooperation between Tajikistan and India in the fields of hydropower, pharmaceuticals, tourism, trade, culture, science, education, setting up joint ventures, building roads, etc.

We are satisfied that the Tajik-Indian relations are developing along an ascending line. However, the existing potential of cooperation between the two countries has not been adequately realised.

Referring to the Tajik-Indian bilateral relations, President of the Republic of Tajikistan Emomali Rahmon stressed:

> "the Republic of Tajikistan within the framework of its bilateral and multilateral relations with India is looking at it as a factor for peace and stability in the region."

I wish to highlight this very aspect, i.e., the possible role of India in promoting peace and security in Central Asia.

Ambassador Rajiv Dogra's speech at the conference about existing problems of the region was right and very relevant. They include the problems of security and drugs coming from Afghanistan. He also mentioned the 'Great Game', which is being played in neighbouring Afghanistan and the Central Asian region in general. I especially liked the fact that Mr. Ambassador looks at these issues from the standpoint of human morality, and most importantly from the standpoint of national interests of the people of Afghanistan. It was, therefore, appropriate for him to ask the question as to how moral it was to continue to play a 'great game', when peaceful people are killed every day?

Undoubtedly, the issues raised by Ambassador Rajiv Dogra about security and drugs are in one way or another connected with Afghanistan. These are most relevant and must be addressed and resolved. However, there is a more important issue, without resolving which it is impossible to guarantee the security in Central Asia and effectively combat drug trafficking. It is imperative, first of all, to normalise the socio-political situation in Afghanistan, with which the security of Central Asia is largely connected.

Unfortunately, the situation in Afghanistan, despite the efforts of the international anti-terrorist coalition, as well as extensive military presence of the West remains critical. Moreover, it has a tendency towards further deterioration and aggravation.

In consideration of this, USA and its Western allies are recently developing a project of peace with the Taliban and are persistently facilitating it. However, in this connection, quite a reasonable question arises. How well thought out is this mechanism, on which the West has pinned such high hopes? Will it not be turned into the next fiasco for them, as it has already been with 'Operation Enduring Freedom' and the plan of the global fight against international terrorism and religious extremism in Afghanistan?

The fact is that, while theoretically it is possible to have peace with the Taliban, which is one of the parties to the Afghan conflict, but in reality there are a number of important factors that give rise to serious doubts about it.

The most interesting thing is that the representatives of the Taliban speak about this quite clearly and unequivocally. Thus, in response to the invitation of the U.S. President on possible talks with 'moderate Taliban', a certain Kari Muhammad Yusuf said on March 10, 2009: "*I do not know what they mean by 'moderate Taliban' and what it means. If they are referring to members who do not fight, and stay at home—talks with them are senseless*".

Still another representative of the Taliban, its press secretary Zabihullah Mojahed was also convinced that: "*There is no moderate Taliban, or supporters of oppressive course. All the Taliban are the same and all are united under the leadership of Mullah Omar*".

However, if contrary to common sense, existent significant factors, as well as the dynamics of the real situation, peace with the Taliban is imposed on the people of Afghanistan, the result will be fraught with several serious dangers not only for Afghanistan itself, but for the entire Central Asian region.

First of all, it would mean the beginning of a new full-scale civil war between the Taliban and pro-Taliban forces in the new government, on one hand and the rest of Afghan society, i.e. numerous national, political and religious forces in Afghanistan, on the other hand.

Secondly, there will be the 'Talibanisation' of the political system of Afghanistan, i.e. militant extremism, radicalism and fanaticism and obscurantism and sectarianism of Taliban will be legitimised.

With such a possible development of the situation in Afghanistan, of course, the threats and challenges coming from this country will grow at an alarming scale, and would negate all the efforts of the international community to combat terrorism, extremism and drug trafficking.

The only correct way out of this situation now in Afghanistan is not peace with the Taliban, but the establishment of legitimate government of national unity that would satisfy all nations and nationalities living in this country.

The Republic of Tajikistan and India can do a lot together in stabilising the situation in Afghanistan and contribute to the resolution of the Afghan question. Especially, they can try to bring closer the geopolitical interests of the states that are involved in Afghanistan.

2

India and Tajikistan: Shared Concerns

Rajiv Dogra

Sometimes the dust of history obscures the shining moments of the past. This reality comes to mind when one views India's relations with Central Asia in general and Tajikistan in particular, especially through the 20th century. The last century was marked by mutual neglect. But why single out the 20th century; because for most of the previous two centuries too the contacts were in a steady decline. Why did this happen? Was it a part of the deliberate policy by the British?

If that indeed was so then what were their motivations? Were they guided by strategic considerations to consciously weaken the Indo-Central Asian links? Perhaps that was indeed the case; and they did so as a part of an astute design. After all that was the time of the Great Game when Russia and the Great Britain were engaged in an intense battle which remains a classic study in the history of diplomatic strategy and espionage. On the other hand could the British have been guided by more base instincts? Was commerce a prime consideration?

Central Asia, it must be remembered, was for long a vital hub of the silk route. Central Asia was also a principal trading partner of India. The British interest in monopolising India's trade with the outer world may well have been a factor, indeed a vital factor, in a calculated game plan to reduce India's traditional trade links with Central Asia.

It could also be argued that Central Asia's southern borders were so remote and largely undefended that it made good strategic sense to isolate this region from global commerce.

Once its trade contacts decreased, the travel to and fro, from Russia and China would have automatically lessened. That would have suited perfectly the British calculations. So this economic ghettoisation of Central Asia may have suited the British in multiple manners. It may or may not have played out precisely along the script that I have now outlined. But the logic of evidence and the tales of history seem to corroborate this.

It was this policy of calculated neglect that led to a virtual drying up of contacts between the two regions. In fact it needed the turn of this millennium for India to make fresh and vigorous efforts to infuse life into a dormant relationship. And the results have been promising already.

However, coming back to the British rule, it is sad to note that a conqueror's strategic considerations should have led to such a pass. But then the same question can also be asked about the Mughal Empire. It is a different thing that the Mughals opted to make India their home and continued in one form or the other to promote contacts between the two regions. And there is ample evidence of that affinity. When you stroll down the bazaars of Dushanbe, the similarities of physique and attire between the women of our Kashmir and them is striking. Obviously then the links are deep rooted.

One more historical connection that comes to mind is that of Babur. It is maintained by some that when young Babur was defeated by his rivals and deprived of his throne, he sought refuge in the mountains overlooking the city of Dushanbe. He spent two years in exile there. It is also said that Babur cogitated on his grand vision of future during his wanderings and soliloquies among those hills; and that he conceived his grand design of conquering Kabul and thereafter the ultimate prize of the crown of India in that two year period.

This is cited by those proficient in regional history as a sign that the idea of Indo-Tajik relations has multiple and interesting roots. But they are quick to add that it was not just a relationship based on history and the esoteric. There was a considerable practical content too in the relationship. That was only natural. If you look at the geographical map of the region you would observe that historically Tajikistan and India were separated at their closest point by the narrow strip of Wakhan corridor which was just about 30 miles wide. This is closer than most cities are to each other.

Regardless of this physical proximity, despite all our similarities and in spite of various claims to multiple links, we seem to have become distant neighbours today. Why is it so? Why is it that despite a desire on both sides to make the relationship thrive, we remain tentative? Why does it give the appearance of an uncertain enterprise fraught with difficulties? Why is there more pessimism than optimism? Why must this be so when the leadership of the two countries, and all the others connected with promoting relationship, declare repeatedly their commitment to a close and ever closer relationship?

Obviously some real difficulties are in the way. If that is the case then it is important to understand their dimensions and by concerted efforts to isolate and remedy the situation. Only then can we hope to optimise the potential that is otherwise there in plenty.

Tajikistan was once a thriving trading post. Khojent in north was one arterial point for the Silk Road. Further down to its south, in the mountains of Badakhshan, lay the other important connection from which yet another branch of the Silk Road wove its way down into India. This was an important source too for trade in semi-precious stones which were found in plenty in the Badakhshan region. As a matter of fact this link to the south was not the only connection of the geographical area that is known today as Tajikistan with India. There was yet another important and highly lucrative trade link. Afghanistan was that link. This link was also the proof of the viability of regional trade. It is a reminder too that the happy experience of the past can be fruitfully replicated.

In Babur's time there were two major trade routes from India to the cities of Central Asia. One passed through Kabul and the other went via Kandahar to Badakhshan, Samarkand, Bukhara and the Ferghana valley. Consequently, Kabul prospered as a major trading centre. According to chroniclers of the period like Clavigo and Hafiz Tanish, the traders of Kabul and Kandahar were not content with profits of 300 or 400 per cent. They earned far greater profits because every year caravans consisting of thousands of horses used to cross Afghanistan transporting goods in either direction.

Bernier for instance records that India provided a huge market for silks, fruits, furs and Central Asian horses while Indian products like white cotton for turbans, tea, spices and pearls were much sought after in the towns of Ferghana and elsewhere in the region.

This commerce must have been vital. It was important enough to have been quoted copiously by the regional scholars and Western observers like Mannuci, Barbra Contarin and Jenkinson. Abul Fazl mentions that there were as many as seven routes used by the traders of Badakhshan to reach Kabul and from there he talks of five practical roads to reach India. As a matter of fact, a 13th century historian Chander Bhan Brahmin too has written about these routes being used by traders from South and Central India. Many of these routes passed through Peshawar and Khyber. Obviously then this trade was lucrative enough to have sustained many towns and it was stable enough to have lasted for several centuries.

One can go on and say that the trade between India and the Central Asian region pre-dates the silk route. After all Alexander would not have ventured so far out of Greece into India had he not heard of the pot of gold that lay here.

However, and regardless of the timeline, it is clear that the logic of regional commerce has been sustained over millennia. It may also not be wide off the mark to make the claim that this regional trade had in some non-formal way anticipated the European Union.

But the question that arises validly then is, why was it that this trade got suspended? If a practice had proved to be beneficial all around why was it put on the back burner? What was the trigger for it? And was there only one reason for this suspension?

It will be unfair to explain this issue only in terms of British self interest or their intransigence. Even if the British had a reason to discourage this once flourishing regional trade why, you might ask, were the links not picked up once the British had packed up from the Indian sub-continent?

That unfortunately is the point where the story becomes starkly obvious. And the simple answer to that question is the venom of Pakistan.

Ever since it's sudden creation, Pakistan has adopted the policy of spiting India even if it involves cutting its own nose. Why else would it have denied India the very basic courtesy of the right of access for its goods to Afghanistan and Central Asia through Pakistani territory? It does not allow the reverse flow of goods either. This transit is the normal procedure sanctioned by International law and practice.

But Pakistan has stubbornly refused to give transit rights to the flow of goods from Tajikistan via the land route into India. Isn't it a worthwhile item of study for a scholar or an institute to calculate for instance the annual loss that Pakistan's action is causing to Tajikistan? Shouldn't some international trade body also interest itself in this violation of International law and take remedial measures? Isn't that what the International practice is all about?

Another connected question is rhetorical and it may interest the future historians, but it is also a question that may hold an important message for us in the region. The question is whether the tragedy of war and strife suffered by Afghanistan since the early eighties would have happened if there had been a thriving regional trade centre in Kabul?

Perhaps the history of Soviet Union itself may have been different if there was greater interchange of goods and people. For Pakistan itself the benefits of free flow of goods to and fro its region may have been immense. It is sometimes said that poverty breeds fundamentalism. Will it be idealistic to assert that had Peshawar prospered, as it did during the centuries of great commerce between India and regions like Badakhshan, perhaps Al Qaeda and Taliban may not have spread in their present virulent form?

Sadly, however, Pakistan's actions have resulted in a regional commerce of an entirely different shape and dimension.

Trade in narcotics, and export of terror, has replaced the commerce in horses and commodities. Afghanistan accounts for a large proportion of the global drug production and Pakistan, through ISI and its Taliban cadres, controls directly or indirectly the bulk of the drug traffic of the world. Sadly, a large proportion of that traffic is channelled through Tajikistan and other Central Asian States.

It will be naïve to assume that with such a large volume of illegal activity the countries through which this trade passes will remain immune from its deleterious effects. The chances are that in some manner or the other it will have a destabilising effect on the society. And there is recent evidence to support this concern.

Some observers maintain that Pakistan's support to the rebels was responsible for the prolongation of the civil war in Tajikistan. It is also alleged that rebel cadres had received training and material support from Pakistan.

There are currently fears among strategic experts that as and when America begins a significant withdrawal of its forces from Afghanistan the ambitions of the Pakistan military and their Taliban surrogates in Afghanistan will once again propel them northwards. A worrying precedent exists to support this view. The Talban had succeeded in their aim when they managed to eliminate the Tajik leader Ahmed Shah Massoud. The next step, the Taliban used to boast then, would see them in Central Asia. It was only after the defeat of the Taliban regime in 2001-02 by USA that these ambitions were thwarted.

Sadly, our region is poised once again on a dangerous edge. The portents are ominous and the future appears to be grim. In that background only an incorrigible romantic will persist with his belief that an uninterruptable and uninterrupted dialogue will somehow solve all the problems. The only thing uninterruptable and uninterrupted in the Pakistani scheme of things is strategic depth. Its instruments of choice to achieve this are sabotage, terror and drugs. We in the region will ignore this reality at our peril.

The West had for long been taken in by Pakistan's double speak.

But now as its costs in Afghanistan and elsewhere in human and material terms increase, it has slowly woken up to the danger that is clear and long term. That's why a former British Prime Minister had alleged that 70 per cent of all terror strikes in U.K. have their origin in Pakistan. Thatis also why the U.S.A. has been adopting an increasingly strident line towards Pakistan. There is some news report or the other every second day which suggests American frustration with Pakistan. But America doesn't just rely on media leaks. It retaliates physically; through strikes like the one on Osama Bin Laden's hide out and through Drone strikes in Pakistani territory aimed at the Al Qaeda and Taliban cadres hiding there.

We in the region have suffered more grievously from terror than any other people or country or region in the world. We have been wounded consistently and for a much longer period of time. Obviously such a climate is not conducive for either economic growth or trade. Ironically, it was our region that had in an earlier era provided to the world the proof of all round prosperity which regional trade can bring. Any realistic assessment of the regional situation today would reveal that while peace, prosperity and progress may still be a desired goal of people but the prognosis is dark and dismal. Pakistan's policies and its actions stand in the way.

Despite these challenges it is still the hope of the people in the region that somehow Afghanistan and Pakistan will stabilise; that the commerce they promote in future will be one of goodwill and not that of hostility. But good wishes alone do not alter belligerent state policy. This, unfortunately, has been the lesson of history from ancient times.

This dilemma is even more acute for neighbours like Tajikistan and India. They have suffered the most from terror and they are likely to remain the principal targets. It is, therefore, in their common interest to align their policies on the strategic front; the earlier this process picks up speed the better because the events in Afghanistan are moving inexorably in none too positive a manner.

However, let's not get stymied by the negatives; there is a world beyond the security concerns too. Here the scope is considerable. It is a pity that trade via the land route is not possible; at least not in the near future. But in today's age there are alternatives to the physical transport of goods.

One possibility that seems practicable is that of investment. If more and more Indian companies were to set up industry in Tajikistan, the economic relationship will grow substantially. If our entrepreneurs could do this in far off Africa, it can surely be done in neighbouring Tajikistan too. But to facilitate this process, Tajikistan would need to pro actively woo them and offer incentives. The two countries would also need to devise a way of predictable and easy mode of travel by commercial airlines. We should be able to visit each other by direct air links. Otherwise, and until the time we are forced to travel via third countries, we will remain distant neighbours.

3

India in the System of International Security of Middle East at the End of 20th – the Beginning of 21st Centuries

Victor Dubovitsky

In a geopolitical picture of the world today, on the boundary of the two millennia, India, undoubtedly, occupies one of the major places, as the largest geopolitical actor in the south of Eurasia. Its formation has occurred in difficult conditions of repartition of the world after the Second World War, disintegration of the colonial system, and the beginning of the formation of ethnocratic states in the countries of Asia and Africa. By the end of the 20th and the beginning of the 21st century, the Republic of India has become an influential country on the world scene possessing a powerful economy, armed forces and an original culture.

However, the region of southern Eurasia, where India is located, is one of the most problematic regions on our planet: inveterate historical grudges, religious conflicts, and also intense struggle of the world powers for its resources, means of communication and strategic points put immense challenges before the leaders of the country. But, as one of the founders of geopolitics, Karl Haushofer has said, 'the country's geography is its destiny!' India has no choice.

The official entry of India into the 'nuclear club' in 1998 became one of the major stages in the emergence of India as the world's largest regional power. It put the country at once on a new level of mutual relations not only with the regional countries, but also in world politics.

The disintegration of the Soviet Union in 1991 became one of the elements of the general process of the destruction of the world order based on the Yalta system that had reflected the outcome of the Second World War. However, a geopolitical warp has been created due to the attempts for the realisation of the globalising project of the world reorganisation and expressed in claims for world leadership by the U.S.A. It does not suit a considerable number of countries, among whom there are many great and regional powers, who have their own views regarding the future world order and also have power and wherewithal to realise their own plans.

In our opinion, while speaking about the geopolitical role of India in the region of Eurasia, it is necessary to consider, first of all, those integration projects in which this country participates. One of the most well-known projects in the Eurasian space is the creation of alliance 'Moscow-Beijing–Delhi', put forward in 1998 by the eminent Russian politician, the great scientist-Orientalist, Evgenie Maksimovich Primakov.

The principal geopolitical basis of such an alliance is the special role of all the three powers—Russia, China and India—both on the continent and in the world as a whole. First of all, it is connected with resources of the above-mentioned states for maintenance of the world and regional security. All of them are nuclear powers with modern, dynamically developing economies and have enormous manpower resources, especially China and India.

The geopolitical basis of this project for Russia became, first, the aversion of the American model of a unipolar world; and second, – the cultivation of political, economic, military-technical and cultural relations with India and China. Thus, the most developed links of Russia by this time have been with India.

It is necessary to underline that all the three participants of the prospective alliance have identical or similar positions on the majority of the most important international problems of modern day, for instance, the formation of the multipolar world; struggle against terrorism; the U.S. aggression against Iraq and threat of application of force against Iran, etc.

However, until recently many political scientists had a clear skepticism concerning the possibility of the allied relations between the two components of the mentioned alliance—China and India. As it is known, there existed a variety of problems between the two powers on the unresolved border dispute and memories of the 1962 border conflict. However, for the last several years the level of relations between these countries has essentially changed. The visit of Indian Prime Minister Vajpayee to China in June 2003, can be considered as the key and significant event in this process. Now the listed problems in the relations between China and India if not resolved completely are in the process of a constructive resolution.

China's support for Pakistan—the major political opponent of India in Southern Asia—has also reduced. For China, Pakistan is becoming a base of Islamic terrorists for separatist organisations from Xinjiang, that has lowered the status of this country in Chinese opinion. This situation is transforming India and China into the eventual allies struggling against the same forces on the territory of Xinjiang and Jammu and Kashmir.

Now the concept of a strategic triangle 'Moscow-Beijing-Delhi' is organically supplemented with the expansion of the alliance by including Iran. In our opinion, the emergence of such a union—Russia-India-China-Iran (RICI)—is capable of providing an effective system of security not only in Central Asia, but also cardinally changing the correlation of geopolitical forces in the world.

The fact of the matter is that Iran, being the key tellurocratic* regional power of the Middle East, simultaneously is one of the leaders of the Islamic world by whom hundreds of millions of Muslims not

*Land-thinking as different from thalassocratic or sea-thinking.

only Shias, but Sunnis as well are guided. With the joining of the strategic triangle 'Moscow-Beijing-Delhi' by such a country as Iran, conditions will pave the way for the creation of a full civilised tellurocratic bloc, representing Slavic-orthodox, Muslim, Confucian-Buddhist and Hindu-Buddhist civilisations. The formation of such a geopolitical bloc of a civilised nature is capable of fundamentally changing the situation on the planet.

The formation of such a geopolitical bloc will inevitably involve into its orbit a number of smaller states of Eurasia connected by bonds of the alliance with four powers mentioned above. As regards Russia, first of all, it concerns the systems Eurasian Economic Community (EurAsEC) and Collective Security Treaty Organisation (CSTO). The 'Satellite' orbit of China will include Laos and Burma and that of India-Nepal, pre-Himalayan princedoms and Sri Lanka. The 'Satellite' orbit of the Islamic Republic of Iran depends on the ideological influence of this country in the Islamic world and, apparently, will capture about 10 states of the Near and Middle East.

The special importance for the earliest creation of such a bloc is the situation in Afghanistan—the main headache of the whole region. It is connected with the forthcoming withdrawal of the American and later of all the western armies from this country by 2014. The U.S. President B. Obama on December 1, 2009 during his speech before teachers and cadets of the military academy in the West-Point declared that by the middle of 2011, U.S. forces would start withdrawing from Afghanistan.

The reason behind such a statement is the actual failure of the American operation 'Enduring Freedom' in Afghanistan that began in October 2001, and later of the whole peace-keeping operation of the West in this country.

The geographic location of Afghanistan in the centre of the Middle East region and also the duration and character of the conflict, into which the ethnic and religious components dominating in the states bordering with Afghanistan, are involved, make the problem of the termination of the conflict one of the most topical one for the whole mankind. The current situation in Afghanistan and likely developments in the near future demand serious analysis of possible challenges and risks for the countries surrounding it.

As regards forecasting the development of the situation in modern Afghanistan, its present condition can be unequivocally characterised as the 'threat' of the second level as per the scale developed by us. 'Threat' denotes the phenomena that may be dangerous to the greatest degree and may be capable of causing substantial loss. They fall directly in the sphere of security and demand immediate active actions in order to neutralise them, including the use of force. They include armed aggression by the states or by non-state actors (international terrorism) and armed actions by ethnic groupings and political organisations, which are in exile. Narco-business and growth in organised crime may also be included in the category of threats.

'Challenges' and 'risks' as geopolitical categories, unlike 'threats', have more indistinct definitions. Thus, the 'challenges' are characterised as "the phenomena affecting the situation, but mainly possessing a destabilising potential. As a rule, the complex of measures of a long-term character are required to respond to them, including economic, political and humanitarian measures". 'Risks' are understood as collateral negative results of economic activities, infringement of the ecological balance, a deterioration of the situation in the water areas of seas, spreading of diseases, for overcoming of which it is required to include amendments into political and economic strategy.

Speaking about the withdrawal of the American armies, it is necessary to consider that such a military-political action connected with transfer of the control over territory to Afghan administrative and military structures, will inevitably lead to the withdrawal of the entire International Security Assistance Force (ISAF) contingent. It is obvious from the analysis of the distribution of efforts in operations in Afghanistan of the armed forces of the various states.

This question became the key one at a meeting of Defence Ministers of the NATO countries in Vilnius in February 2008, when Canada, whose contingent is in one of the most problematic areas of southern Afghanistan (Kandahar), threatened to withdraw forces if allies did not increase their presence. A number of countries, notably,

Germany, France and Italy—whose armies operate in quieter provinces—were extremely reluctant to give their units for support of the British, Canadian, Netherlands and Danish military men operating in the most dangerous southern provinces.

This question was discussed with a big sharpness in Vilnius where Robert Gates had declared that the alliance of 26 states 'was divided in two parts', one of which is ready 'to battle and die for freedom of the people', and another was not. The difference in the contribution for conducting operations of various countries of NATO was also noted during the anniversary summit of the organisation in Strasbourg-Kele on April, 3-4, 2009, when its participants noticed "the absence of positive results of the activity of international forces in Afghanistan that speaks about the default by the allies of their obligations for allocation of enough resources to the structure of International forces for the Security Promotion". By the end of June 2010 the aggregate number of ISAF contingent had reached 120,000 people and had exceeded the number of the Soviet armies in Afghanistan during the period 1979-1989 (The maximum—108 thousand).

In our opinion, the withdrawal of troops will be made in the short term which may not exceed one year as the longer stay in Afghanistan of a decreasing contingent of armed forces of the Western countries will inevitably lead to a sharp rise in losses. Of course, in comparison with losses of the Soviet armed forces in 1979-1989, they do not look so high, however, the modern Western society, formed on the philosophy of hedonism, is not ready to accept even comparatively smaller losses of lives. At the end of 2009, losses of the anti-Taliban coalition (since October 2001) looked as follows: 1,296 people were killed, out of them—746 military men of the U.S. army and 550 – from other Western countries. By the end of June 2010, these losses increased to 1,879 persons, two thirds of whom belong to the American military. Losses of the Afghan army for this period have made up 11,152 people. Besides, losses among the civilian population of Afghanistan—7,589 people.

Thus, it seems more likely that the conditions in Afghanistan may lead to the renewal of the civil war, the basic participants of which will be, in our opinion, not the Western forces, aspiring to construct the democratic society and Talibs but ethno-territorial grouping of Pashtuns, on the one hand and the bloc of the Central Asian ethnoses and Hazaras, on the other hand. The first of them (considering the number of Pashtuns, living in the zone of free tribes in Pakistan) will reach 20-27 million people, the second one from 10.5 to 14 million. In the process of aggravation of internal struggle and disorder of the remaining Westernised state structures, there will be a split on the lines of the above-mentioned divide in all public institutes and, first of all—in the Afghan National Army. By analogy to the period 1989-1992, when there was the degradation of the Najibullah regime supported by the USSR, each of the two contradictory forces will receive its share of the trained military men, arms and equipment. After that having legitimately formed military-political blocs, they will enter into a fierce struggle.

The Pashtun grouping will support preservation of the integrity of the national (read - Pashtun) statehood and territorial integrity of the present territory of Afghanistan while the other grouping—having recreated a new variant of 'Northern Alliance', will begin the struggle for upholding the independence of the territory, occupied by ethnoses comprising it. This process, depending on the speed of the withdrawal of the Western armies, will take from one to one and a half years. Such a development of the situation, undoubtedly, is of serious concern for the surrounding countries. What combination of measures of a long-term character should these countries take in response to the situation in Afghanistan?

Creation of the updated 'Northern Alliance' and active military actions with the Pashtun bloc will demand constant and expensive intervention of the states surrounding Afghanistan into the process as it was in 1996-2001. The main burden of military and economic support of the bloc will again fall on Tajikistan, Iran, Uzbekistan and, possibly, Turkmenistan. From the great world powers the help of Russia will be required.

The new geopolitical situation which has developed in the south of Eurasia with creation of SCO (2001) and CSTO (2003), and also more and more intense situation in Xinjiang, will also result in bringing China to the ranks of allies of 'Northern alliance'. Such development of the situation seems to be even more likely in view of considerable warming of Chinese-Indian relations in 2004-2009.

During such a development of the situation around Afghanistan, on India's shoulders will be put a difficult and responsible task of consolidating all the constructive forces of the southern sub-region of Eurasia in the struggle against political and religious extremism. In our opinion, India possesses both the resources and political will for this purpose and is capable of meeting any challenges and risks in the zone of its geopolitical responsibility.

4

India and Tajikistan: Common Concerns and Shared Interests in Evolving Regional Geopolitics

Jyotsna Bakshi

Situated on the cross-roads of major empires and trade routes, Central Asia has always been the meeting ground and an area of cross-fertilisation of diverse cultures. Although views differ as to what constitutes the exact geographical parameters of Central Asia, still in contemporary international politics the reference to Central Asia generally means the five former Soviet Central Asian republics. Thus, Kazakhstan, Kyrgyzstan, Tajikistan, Turkmenistan and Uzbekistan are grouped together as a distinct geographical sub-region. They are called 'CARs' (Central Asian Republics), 'Central Asian states' or 'stans'. The region is extremely rich in human as well as natural resources. The interests of all the major powers and various regional players are deeply involved in the region both because of its geo-strategic location in the heart of Eurasia and abundant natural resources.

The Central Asian states are a part of India's extended and strategic neighbourhood. India and Central Asia have maintained extensive and deep civilisational contacts spanning thousands of years. The mountains that separate Central Asia from the Indian subcontinent have never been an insurmountable barrier in the way of interaction of the people of the two neighbouring regions. In the course of centuries, a dense cultural and ethnic intermingling took place between the people of the Indian subcontinent and Central Asia. The developments in Central Asia have always impacted on India in the past and may do so in future again.

Of all the Central Asian states, Tajikistan is physically the closest to the Indian subcontinent. Only a narrow strip of Afghan territory called the Wakhan corridor separates Tajikistan from the northern most parts of the Indian subcontinent. The western strip of Wakhan corridor is just 13 to 25 km wide (the widest part of the corridor is 65 km). I of was told during my visit to the Gorno-Badakhshan region of Tajikistan that people could cross the corridor on foot in three days and reach the northern areas of the Indian subcontinent.

In ancient times, the merchants from 'Sogdiana' or Sugd, which included parts of present day Tajikistan, were most active in promoting India-Central Asia trade, spreading Buddhism and in cross-fertilisation of Indo-Central Asian cultures. The southern branch of the historic East-West route connected India and Central Asia. This route was also called 'cotton and precious goods route'. Until the 19th century a flourishing trade took place between India and Central Asia. However, trade declined after India went under British colonialism and the Tsarist Russian Empire expanded into Central Asia. The two biggest imperialist powers—Tsarist Russia and Britain—were locked in the famous 'great game' in the second half of the 19th century and the early 20th century for control over Afghanistan and Central Asia. Finally, Britain and Tsarist Russia decided not to cross ways and turned Afghanistan into a buffer state. According to the treaty of 1907, it was agreed that the narrow strip of Afghan territory—the Wakhan corridor—would be separating the British Indian possessions and the Tsarist possession of Central Asia. Following the October 1917 Soviet Revolution, the ideological and political antagonism between the British colonial regime and the Soviet Union came in the way of wider interaction between the people of the two regions. The contacts were revived after India got Independence in 1947. With the warming up of Indo-Soviet ties, Indian economic and cultural influence was allowed to penetrate in Central Asia even during the Soviet period.

The emergence of independent states in Central Asia following the disintegration of the Soviet Union has opened up vast new opportunities for the expansion of multi-faceted ties between the Central Asian states and India.

India-Tajikistan Ties

Because of geographical proximity and common threat perceptions, the Republic of Tajikistan occupies top priority in India's overall approach to Central Asia. Diplomatic ties were established between India and Tajikistan on August 28, 1992. Since then India-Tajikistan cooperation has grown in all fields. Tajikistan—like all other Central Asian states—follows a balanced multi-vector policy. Since 2002, Tajik foreign policy is officially described as 'open doors policy' based on cooperation with all countries on the basis of mutual respect, friendship and benefit. India occupies a central position in South Asia and the Indian Ocean region. It is a bastion of stability in an otherwise troubled and turbulent neighbourhood. Close cooperation with India may strengthen the important southern leg of Tajikistan's multi-vector policy.

India-Tajikistan bilateral cooperation encompasses a broad spectrum from political, economic, cultural and military fields to education, science and technology and academic and humanitarian spheres. Visits by leaders of the two countries have helped in developing close personal contact and rapport at the highest level. President Emomali Rahmon of Tajikistan visited India several times—in 1995, 1999, 2001 and 2006. President Rahmon's latest visit to India was on September 3, 2012. It was decided during the visit to further cement India-Tajikistan relations by raising them to the level of 'strategic partnership'.

In 2003, then Indian Prime Minister Atal Bihari Vajpayee visited Tajikistan, which was a landmark visit. The first Presidential visit from India to Tajikistan was undertaken by Pratibha Devisingh Patil from September 6-8, 2009. This reflected the growing importance India attaches to ties with Tajikistan.

There has been continuous exchange of visits by Ministers of Foreign Affairs of the two countries and other dignitaries that have bolstered mutual cooperation. By 2007, the two countries had signed 30 interstate, intergovernmental and interdepartmental treaties and agreements at different levels of government. On July 31, 2009, the two countries signed the agreement to avoid double taxation in order to bolster the flow of technology, investment and services.

Common faith in liberal pluralism, secularism and tolerance characterises abiding friendship and mutual trust between India and Tajikistan. Both the countries stand for moderation and modernisation as against extremist and obscurantist ideologies like religious fundamentalism and fanaticism. These ideologies have considerable following in neighbouring Pakistan and Taliban-dominated areas of Afghanistan.

Common Stake in Regional Peace and Stability for Continued Economic Growth

India and Tajikistan have a vital stake in peace and stability in the entire region in order to maintain and further accelerate their economic growth. Indian economy is the second fastest growing economy in the world. By PPP standard, India is the fourth largest economy in the world. It is one of the four fastest growing economies known as BRIC countries (Brazil, Russia, India and China).[1] By the middle of the present century, the Indian economy is projected to become the third largest economy in the world (see figure 1 below). Despite numerous difficulties and obstacles, Tajikistan has also registered impressive economic growth in the past decade. Between2004 to 2009, the GDP of Tajikistan registered about seven per cent growth rate annually (see figure 2 below).

Although the growth rate was from an earlier low base as the Tajik economy was completely devastated by the civil war from 1992 to 1997, still, the figures present an optimistic picture. The economies of both India and Tajikistan are on a growth trajectory. Both the countries need peace to maintain the tempo of economic growth.

Figure 1: The Largest Economies in 2050

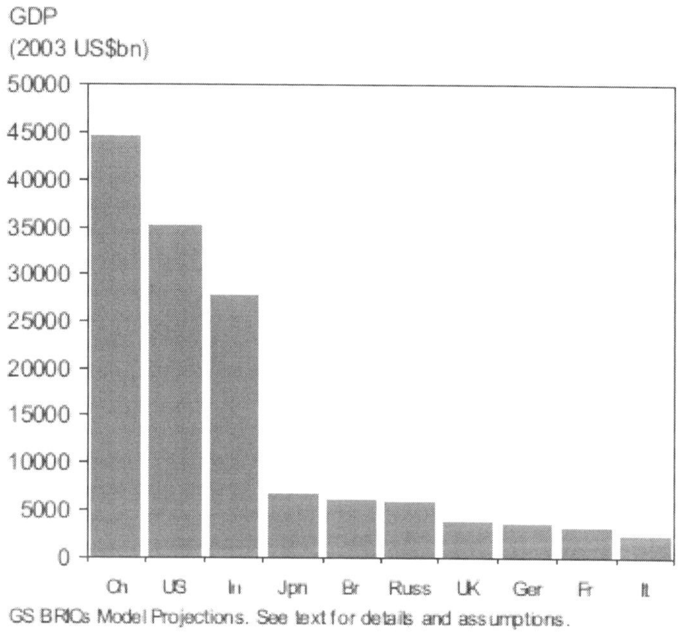

Source: Goldman Sachs, *Dreaming With the BRICS: The Path to 2050*, Global Economics Paper 99.

Figure 2: GDP Growth Rate of Tajikistan

Year	*GDP—real growth rate*
2003	5.00%
2004	7.00%
2005	10.50%
2006	6.70%
2007	7.00%
2008	7.80%
2009	7.90%
2010	3.40%

Source: http://www.indexmundi.com/tajikistan/gdp_real_growth_rate.html

Common Concerns and Threat Perceptions

Religious extremism and terrorism pose a common threat to the two countries as indeed to all the countries of the region. Both India and Tajikistan are victims of these forces and have suffered incalculable losses in this battle. It is estimated that more than 50,000 precious lives were lost in the Tajik Civil War between government forces and Islamic opposition forces from 1992 to 1997. About 1.2 million people were internally displaced during the Civil War in Tajikistan. Thousands of people have been killed in terrorist violence in the northern Indian state of Jammu and Kashmir and other parts of India. Nevertheless, it is important to highlight that both India and Tajikistan have displayed exemplary will and strength and have not succumbed to these forces. The struggle against these forces still continues. The threat of terrorism emanates from the troubled Af-Pak region in the common neighbourhood of both India and Tajikistan.

India and Tajikistan live in a dangerous neighbourhood of strife-torn Afghanistan. Tajikistan shares a more than 1,200-km long border with Afghanistan. Practically, India is Afghanistan's near neighbour. Vital security interests of both countries are affected by the developments in Afghanistan. Al Qaeda and Taliban militants are well entrenched in the adjacent tribal areas of Pakistan where the writ of the Pakistan government does not run. The southern and south-eastern parts of Afghanistan bordering on Pakistan are reeling under constant turmoil due to Taliban insurgency.

Owing to continued conflict, lawlessness, lack of governance, grinding poverty and widespread unemployment, poppy cultivation has become the main vocation of the people especially in Taliban-infested southern parts of Afghanistan. Afghanistan accounts for more than 90 percent of the opium poppy production of the world[2] and drug money is financing the Taliban militancy.[3] Neighbouring countries—including Tajikistan and other Central Asian states, have become major drug transit routes to European markets.[4] Drug trafficking is adversely affecting the socio-economic health and stability of the polity of neighbouring countries.

The experience of the Taliban rule in Afghanistan from 1996 to 2001 has been most dismal for the people of Afghanistan and alarming for neighbouring countries. The Taliban militia imposed inhumane medieval code of justice to the shock and horror of the entire world. The treatment of women was abominable. There were mass massacres of minority ethnic groups. The Central Asian states, Russia, India and Iran at that time supported the Northern Alliance in Afghanistan that was fighting against the Taliban. India built a hospital in Farkhor, Tajikistan in support of the Northern Alliance. It was to this hospital that the famous Afghan Tajik leader Ahmed Shah Masoud was rushed after being fatally wounded in September 2001 by Al Qaeda suicide bombers in the garb of photo journalists.

Afghanistan under the Taliban had turned into a haven for all terrorist and extremist forces. From their bases in Afghanistan the Islamic Movement of Uzbekistan (IMU) carried out militant activities in the Central Asian states of Tajikistan, Kyrgyzstan and Uzbekistan in the years 1999-2001. IMU's objective was to establish an Islamic Caliphate in the populous and fertile Fergana Valley[5] region of Central Asia and from there further expand their influence. Cross-border terrorist attacks were also carried out extensively in the northern Indian state of Jammu and Kashmir and other areas by militant groups supported by Pakistan and Taliban-controlled Afghanistan. The terrorists posed a critical challenge to Indian security and its secular and democratic system.

A close nexus existed between the Taliban on the one hand and Pakistan's military and its intelligence service Inter Services Intelligence (ISI). A mere Islamic students' militia that the Taliban was, could make such spectacular military gains in Afghanistan only with the full backing from Pakistan Army and ISI. Scholars and experts around the world, including Pakistani scholars like Ahmed Rashid, have extensively written and commented on the links between Taliban and Pakistani establishment dominated by the Army.[6] The well-known objective of Pakistan's military-political establishment was—and continues to this day—the establishment of a surrogate pro-Pakistan regime in Afghanistan in order to acquire so-called 'strategic depth' against India.[7]

Despite controlling Kabul and a large part of Afghan territory between 1996 and 2001, the Taliban remained an international pariah. Its medieval obscurantist ideology, judicial system, travesty of human rights, suppression of women and minorities caused widespread indignation. Pakistan, Saudi Arabia and UAE were the only three countries that recognised the Taliban.

The Taliban were defeated and removed from power in October 2001 by the U.S.-led war on terror 'Operation Enduring Freedom' following the 9/11 terror attacks on the U.S. by Al Qaeda, which received sanctuary in Afghanistan along with other terror groups. Under intense U.S. pressure, Pakistan's President General Musharraf (1999-August 2008) made a policy about-turn, severed ties with Taliban, and joined the U.S.-led global war on terror. The U.S. also accorded Pakistan the status of Major Non-NATO Ally in 2004 in view of Pakistan's geopolitical importance as supply route for U.S. and NATO troops operating in land-locked Afghanistan.

Following their defeat, the remnants of Taliban and Al Qaeda took refuge in the tribal regions of Pakistan bordering on Afghanistan. Since then a slow Talibanisation of Pakistan has been taking place. The entire world knows today that amidst talks of international solidarity in the war against terror, a part of Pakistani security establishment continues to maintain links with terrorist elements and aid their anti-India and anti-Afghan activities. The ISI continued to maintain ties with Taliban militants. The 'Double game' of Pakistan has been exposed by scholars and experts around the world. Vladimir Plastun, a noted Russian expert of Oriental Studies, for instance, remarked, "Pakistan cannot decide whether it wants to fight terrorism or encourage it as state policy." Former advisor to the U.S. President on Middle East and South Asia, Bruce Riedel (Senior Fellow at the Brookings Institute), writes,

> "Pakistan has become the most dangerous country in the world....It is the epicentre of the global jihadist movement that attacked New York in 2001 and Mumbai in 2008. Its weak civilian government may have good intentions but seems powerless to address the country's multiple crises. The Army remains the patron of parts of the jihadist Frankenstein even as it fights other parts of the monster. The ongoing revelations of David Hedley on the ISI's role in Mumbai 26/11 only underscore how dangerous Pakistan is today."[8]

No wonder, the chief of Al Qaeda—the world's most dreaded terrorist organisation—Osama bin Laden, was found living in Abbotabad in Pakistan, which is a garrison town of the Pakistani Army. Laden was killed in a covert operation by the USA. Recently, Admiral Mike Mullen of the USA openly accused Pakistani spy agency ISI of having links with the militants.[9] Pakistan's military-political establishment dominated by the powerful Army continues to follow the policy of hunting with the hound and running with the hare. On the one hand it is the ally of the international coalition forces fighting terrorism, on the other hand, it is giving support and sanctuary to the very same terrorist forces that are fighting against the coalition forces.

Despite the presence of U.S. and NATO troops, the Taliban insurgency has grown in Afghanistan in recent years. There is a growing desire among the Western countries—including the USA, to seek a face-saving agreement with the Taliban insurgents that may facilitate an early exit from the Afghan quagmire. In December 2009, President Obama announced the increase of 30,000 U.S. troops in Afghanistan in order to be able to defeat or subdue Taliban insurgents and negotiate with them from a position of strength. Simultaneously, he set the time line for the withdrawal of troops from Afghanistan beginning with July 2011. It has been decided to withdraw troops by 2014. The situation in Afghanistan today remains extremely fluid and uncertain.

Best possible solution of Afghan crisis: Given the best case scenario, Afghanistan can emerge as a land bridge connecting Central Asia, South Asia and the Middle East and facilitate increased trade and commerce, which may lead to regional peace and prosperity. To make it a reality, it is important that all the major powers and regional players join hands to promote peace, stability and economic development of Afghanistan. This would serve the best interests of India and neighbouring Central Asian states, particularly Tajikistan as the latter shares a long border with Afghanistan. What is more, it would provide succour to the long suffering people of Afghanistan. There is greater readiness on the part of the USA and its Western allies to enlist the support of Russia and the Central Asian states in the effort to stabilise Afghanistan. In view of increasing attacks on trucks taking supplies to U.S.-NATO troops in Afghanistan that pass through Pakistan territory, an attempt is being made to operationalise the Northern Distribution Networks (NDN) across Russia and the Central Asian states.

According to latest reports, the USA is rapidly expanding the aerial and Central Asian routes to ensure supplies for U.S. and NATO forces in Afghanistan. U.S. military planners are seeking to raise the share of NDN to 75 percent by the end of 2011.[10] With the construction of the bridge on the river Pyanj between Tajikistan and Afghanistan, the former has become an important country for supplies to Afghanistan.

On its part, India is one of the largest donors to Afghanistan having already donated more than $2.3 billion aid to the latter.[11] It is running a number of projects for reconstruction and socio-economic development of Afghanistan. India is also training in a big way Afghan professionals in various skills. The Afghan students constitute the largest contingent studying in various Indian universities under the Indian Council for Cultural Relations (ICCR) fellowship programme. In 2007, Afghanistan became a member of South Asian Association for Regional Cooperation (SAARC). As a bastion of stability and engine of growth in South Asia, India can play a major role in the stabilisation and nation-building of Afghanistan. Afghanistan is also invited as a guest to the summits of Shanghai Cooperation Organisation (SCO), of which China, Kazakhstan, Kyrgyzstan, Russia, Tajikistan and Uzbekistan are members and India along with Pakistan, Iran and Mongolia are observers.

Likely Worst Case Scenario: Continued strife and bloodshed in Afghanistan and its further descent into chaos followed by the precipitous exit of the International Security Assistance Force (ISAF) led by the USA might be the worst case scenario that may adversely affect the peace and stability of the entire region. The Pakistani Army's game plan of seeking 'strategic depth' and imposing a compliant pro-Pakistan regime in Afghanistan may lead to the return of the nightmarish situation there that existed between 1996-2001.

Possible Middle Case Scenario: The middle case scenario may imply continued competition and rivalry among great powers and various regional players accompanied by partial cooperation to prevent uncontrolled chaos and destabilisation of the entire region. The 'great game' may continue in new garb reflecting conflicting ambitions and interests.

In all these scenarios, close strategic cooperation between India and Tajikistan is crucial for protecting vital security interests of both the countries. Being situated in the neighbourhood of the strife-torn Af-Pak region, they are likely to be most affected by continued turmoil and conflict in this area and its likely adverse fallout.

India and Tajikistan: Shared Interests and Growing Cooperation

The national interests of India and Tajikistan largely coincide in the current scenario. India understands the challenges to the Tajik security posed by extremist and militant forces in the neighbourhood and strongly supports its independence and territorial integrity. Similarly, a strong and stable India in South Asia remains a bulwark of peace and security in the entire region. Both the countries support each other's efforts to maintain peace and stability in their respective countries and in the region as a whole.

The people and government of Tajikistan have displayed great wisdom and far sight by concluding a peace accord with the opposition forces and ending the civil war thereby restoring peace and unity in the country. India warmly welcomed the end of civil war in Tajikistan and restoration of peace and extended all possible help in the peace process. The success of national reconciliation in Tajikistan marked the triumph of Tajik nationalism. India and Tajikistan have established a Joint Working Group on Counter Terrorism. India also provides training to Tajikistan's young professionals, diplomats and defence personnel to help in the nation and state building process. According to figures available in mid-2010, more than 75 Tajik military cadets and 43 defence officers have already undergone training at India's National Defence Academy (NDA) and Indian Military Academy (IMA) respectively. Every year the Indian Council for Cultural

Relations (ICCR) gives 30 scholarships to young scholars of Tajikistan to pursue higher studies in various Indian universities. So far more than 250 Tajik students have received ICCR scholarships. Every year 100 young professionals of Tajikistan get training under the Indian Technical and Economic Cooperation (ITEC) programme. So far more than 700 Tajik personnel have received professional training under ITEC. During President Rahmon's September 2012 visit, it has been decided to raise ITEC slots for Tajikistan to 150 annually. The two countries are cooperating in education, science and technology.

Tajikistan supports India's claim for permanent membership of the UNSC. Along with Russia and other Central Asian states, Tajikistan has consistently favoured that India becomes a full-fledged member of Shanghai Cooperation Organisation.

The Importance of Transport Connectivity

Transport connectivity may lead to increased trade, business cooperation and people-to-people contacts between the two countries. Geography has destined Tajikistan to become a hub of important transport corridors linking South Asia with Central Asia and East Asia. The landlocked mountainous Republic of Tajikistan had until recently remained isolated from major trade and transport arteries. During the Soviet period it was linked with the northward routes only—with Kyrgyzstan, Uzbekistan and Turkmenistan and further with Russian metropolis. Now Tajikistan is already realising its long-cherished dream of being connected with countries in all four directions as the following Asian Highway map demonstrates (Map 1).

On August 26, 2007 the important bridge between Tajikistan and Afghanistan was inaugurated by the Presidents of the two countries. The bridge opens the way for further linking Tajikistan to countries of the Indian subcontinent via Afghanistan. Earlier, in May 2004, the Kulma Pass border that links Tajikistan with the Xinjiang region of China was opened. The Indian-built Zaranj-Delaram road provides access to land-locked Afghanistan and Central Asian states to the Iranian port of Chabahar and further to the Indian ports on the western coast (Map 2).

Map 1: Asian Highway Routes in Tajikistan

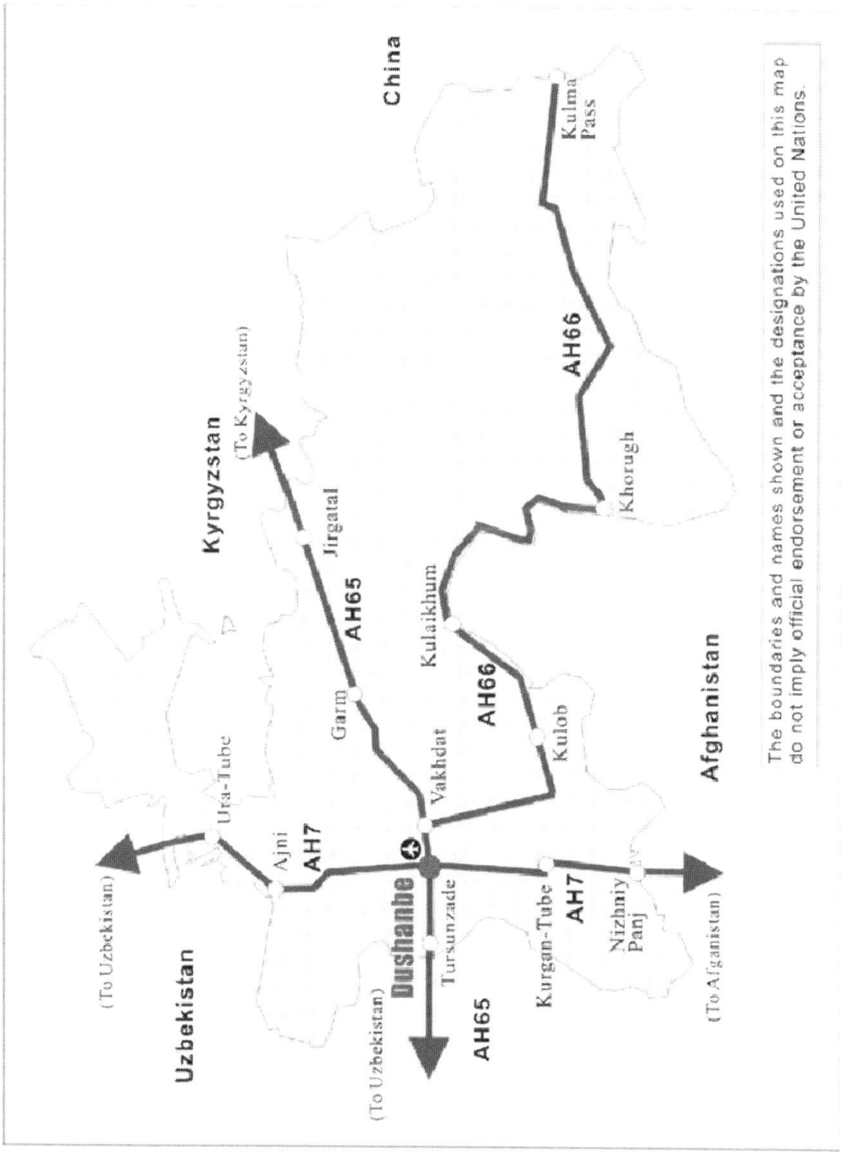

Map 2

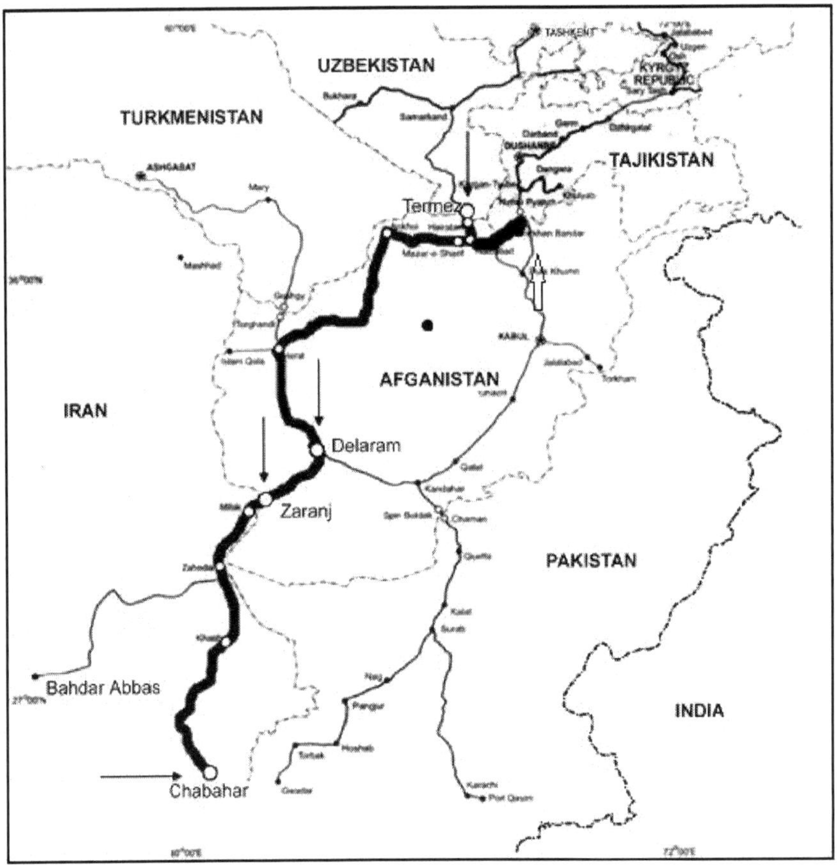

- Actual implementation of the rules and admission of new members by consensus may take some time.

The shortest route from Central Asia to South Asia lies through Afghanistan and Pakistan. India has taken several initiatives for improving ties with Pakistan so that this route is opened for movement of goods and people. India stands for maintaining the present political map and not change the borders, but making the borders soft so that there is free flow of trade and increased people-to-people contacts. In order to make it possible, it is important to isolate and defeat the terror groups and break the nexus between the terror groups and their supporters within Pakistani military and its Inter-Services Intelligence (ISI). Within Pakistan also—despite the traditional domination of the military establishment, a peace constituency is slowly emerging that wishes to benefit from enhanced trade with India. This gives hope for the future. If this opinion further strengthens and has its way in Pakistan, it will bring peace and prosperity not only to South Asia, but also boost cooperation between the countries of South Asia and Central Asia. This, indeed, would be the best case scenario that would serve the interests and aspirations of the peoples of the two neighbouring regions.

NOTES

1. Beginning with the first summit of BRIC leaders at Yekaterinburg (Russia) on June 16, 2009, the four countries have been holding annual summits. In December 2010, South Africa formally joined BRIC nations, which became BRICS.
2. http://www.voanews.com/policy/editorials/Poppy-Production-In-Afghanistan-87715832.html, March 14, 2010.
3. http.//www.humansecuritygateway.com/documents/NAF_FinancingtheTaliban_TracingtheDollars.pdf
4. Aleksandr Bogatik and Yelena Sorokina, "Central Asia remains main Afghan narcotrafficking route," at CentralAsiaOnline.com, September 16, 2010.
5. Fergana Valley was divided by Stalin between Uzbekistan, Kyrgyzstan and Tajikistan.
6. Ahmed Rashid: *Taliban: Islam, Oil and the New Great Game in Central Asia* (London; I.B. Tauris Publishers, 2001 edition, *passim.*
7. Jyotsna Bakshi, "Pakistan's Geopolitical Game Plan in Afghanistan", *Himalayan and Central Asian Studies,* Vol. 1, No. 2, July-September 1997. General Mirza Aslam Beg, Pakistani army chief from 1988-1991, was the first to coin the term "strategic depth" regarding Pakistan's ambitions in Afghanistan. This view of Pakistan's ambitions and designs *vis-à-vis* Afghanistan is widely shared by scholars and analysts around the world. See, for instance, Peter Marsden: *Afghanistan, Aid, Armies & Empires,* I.B. Tauris, London, New York (South Asian Edition, 2010), p. 82.
8. *Times of India,* October 30, 2010.
9. http://www.bbc.co.uk/news/world-south-asia-13153538, April 21, 2011.
10. Craig Whitlock, "US Alters, Expands Afghan Supply Routes", *Washington Post,* July 3, 2011.
11. During his visit to Afghanistan in May 2011, Indian Prime Minister Manmohan Singh announced the grant of another $500 million aid to Afghanistan.

5

The Indian Factor in the Geopolitical Realities of Central Asia

G.M. Maytdinova

At present times India is a recognised centre of power in South Asia and one of the major actors, which has great political weight in the system of international relations of the 21st century. The role of the Central Asian factor in India's foreign policy in recent decades has increased significantly. This is due to increased geopolitical importance of the region, especially following the emergence of new sovereign states in the former Soviet Union and the formation of the new model of international relations in this territory. The continued destabilising role of the Afghan situation located between the borders of India and Central Asia further underscores the significance of Central Asia in Indian foreign policy. The northern most part of India is partially located in Central Asia. It is in India's interest to have closer communication and energy links as well as general intensification of economic and cultural cooperation with countries in the region.

There are many common points in the historical fate of the two macro-regions—Central Asia and South Asia. The historical experience of ethnic, economic and cultural interaction between people of the

Indian subcontinent and Central Asia (post-Soviet Central Asia) spans over several thousand years. The highest manifestation of the Central Asian-Indian political and cultural synthesis was the evolution of common Kushan civilisation. Buddhism that spread from India to Central Asia since the beginning of our era played an important role in the history of the Tajik people up to 9th century. In addition, considerable experience of good neighbourly relations—accumulated over decades of Indo-Soviet cooperation—provides new impetus for cooperation. India has significant advantages compared with other political actors in Central Asia as interstate relations with India are not burdened by the negative historical memory and there is a positive historical experience of co-development of unified state formation in ancient times. At the present stage, India does not represent for new states of the region ideological, demographic or territorial threat.

At the beginning of the new millennium, one major step that India took in the Central Asian vector was the initiative of the 'New Silk Road of Indian foreign policy', in the course of implementation of which it was able to reach an understanding with the leaders of Central Asian countries on harmonisation of positions on a particular range of international issues, like, maintenance of peace, settlement of regional conflicts, countering terrorism and separatism and the fight against drug trafficking, etc.

One of the main foreign policy goals of India in Central Asia is to prevent the spread and consolidation in the region of militant Islamic fundamentalism. India sees the Central Asian states as a 'buffer zone' to curb the international religious fundamentalism. India has also sought to prevent the one-sided influence of Pakistan in the region. The latter has widely used the Islamic factor to achieve its foreign policy goals. In this context, the main task of India in the region is to prevent the formation of any alliance hostile to India.

The entry of new states in the region into the ranks of the Non-Aligned Movement (NAM) was a favourable development for India as India plays a leading role in the movement. Turkmenistan and Uzbekistan have already become full members of NAM, while Tajikistan, Kyrgyzstan and Kazakhstan act as observers.

At the same time, India is actively participating in the Conference on Interaction and Confidence-Building Measures in Asia (CICA) and is an observer in the Shanghai Cooperation Organisation (SCO). On their part, the Central Asian states support the candidature of India as a permanent member of U.N. Security Council. They also support the entry of India and Pakistan in the SCO as full members.

The development of India's relations with Central Asia is conducive to the mutual interests of the parties in resolving issues of regional security, the Afghan settlement, the fight against religious extremism, terrorism and drug trafficking. A particular danger to Central Asia as well as India lies in the penetration of terrorists and religious extremists from Afghanistan and their militant activities. In this regard, in 2003-2005, India concluded bilateral agreements with Tajikistan, Kazakhstan, Uzbekistan and Kyrgyzstan on cooperation in countering terrorism, providing for the establishment of joint anti-terrorist groups, sharing experiences, conducting joint exercises and training of armed forces personnel from these states in India.[1]

Problems and Challenges before Central Asian Region

Central Asia at present is facing a serious impact of geopolitical factors that might impede the implementation of national interests of countries of the region. These are, problems related to water issues and of transboundary rivers, supply of energy by certain countries, transport and communication system using the transit potential of neighbouring states, settlement of border issues between neighbouring countries, the difference in levels of economic development, customs barriers, visa and border crossing regime, poor transportation infrastructure, weak economic ties between the countries of the region, extreme poverty of the population, corruption, parochialism, increasing deterioration in the development of agriculture and industry, the ever-increasing outflow of able-bodied population, environmental degradation, etc. They tend to threaten regional stability. In addition, there are nontraditional security threats, such as international terrorism, religious extremism, separatism, interethnic conflicts, clandestine drug trafficking and illegal movement of weapons.[2] In the 21st century international drugs trade has begun to play a more significant role in Central Asia.

Ethno-political Issues in Fergana Valley

In the Fergana Valley, the interests of Tajikistan, Kyrgyzstan and Uzbekistan are involved in the field of distribution of water and energy resources and the issues of border settlement. There are problems like the influence of the Islamic factor, the aggravation of inter-ethnic and intra-ethnic relations, drug trafficking, illegal migration, organised crime, corruption, demography, etc. that are all interrelated. The above-mentioned problems in conjunction with the predominant poverty of the population are creating here a major conflict node, which –along with the destabilising influence of the Afghan factor—is capable of blowing up the stability of Central Asia. Analysing the situation in Fergana Valley, it can be concluded that if there is a threat to the sovereignty of one of the three states that share the Valley, then it should be seen as a threat to the whole Central Asian region. There remains a situation of internal conflict within the triangle of Tajikistan-Uzbekistan-Kyrgyzstan. It is clear that a number of large-scale and local permanent conflict situations may affect the development of the region in the near future.

Rivalry of the Leading Powers with Geopolitical and Geo-economic Interests in the Region

It may be argued that just a struggle for energy resources and control over communications in the region can pave the way for transformation of Central Asia into one of the crisis corners of the world in the coming years and make actual the military threat to the national security of the new states, along with the existing non-traditional threats.[3]

Major world powers involved in big politics in Central Asia seek to realise their national interests. The USA has a major stake in ending the hostilities in Afghanistan, but at the same time is seeking to maintain a military presence there in order to remain a key player in this part of the world for a long time. E.U. aims to establish links with Central Asian countries, which are rich in oil and gas, in the hope of obtaining access to the resources of Central Asia. E.U. is forced to participate in the Afghan military campaign led by the United States, partly to finance it and to provide troops as part of NATO forces to help Washington. China waits, preferring to focus attention and efforts on the stability in the Xinjiang Uighur Autonomous Region, where there are increased tensions. The basic goal of Russia—as it has been officially stated by government—is to reduce the huge drug trafficking from the Afghan provinces to Russia's regions. In other words, the main tasks of the participants coincide only marginally.[4]

The Militarisation and Increased Conflict Potential in Afghanistan

Despite the fact that the international coalition and NATO have contributed to the military containment of the 'Taliban' and to the development of Afghanistan, they could not radically change the difficult situation in the country. Afghanistan has long become a centre of international terrorism, religious extremism, organised crime, drug trafficking, arms smuggling, and illegal migration. The aggravation of ethno-political problems gives new impetus to the Afghan conflict. In fact, in Afghanistan there is a conflict of many ethnic elite groups, especially complicated by outside interference. Foreign troops from 41 countries are operating on the government side in Afghanistan. Twenty eight foreign military bases have been established in the country. The militarisation of the country, existing ethnic and political problems and the concentration of destructive forces, have become a source of threats not only to regional but also global security.

Since the beginning of the first decade of the 21st century, stability in Central Asia increasingly depends on near catastrophic situation established in the region due to the long political and military conflict in Afghanistan. The U.S. campaign against terrorism has become a new cause of intensification of terrorist groups, the manifold increase in the production of drugs, illegal migration, arms trafficking and other threats to the security of both Afghanistan and all countries of the Eurasian continent. This calls for active response from the neighbours of Afghanistan, for whom the Afghan settlement is vital.[5]

The most important actors with influence in Afghanistan are the USA and NATO, EU, Pakistan, Iran, China, Russia, the countries of Central Asia (Tajikistan, Uzbekistan, and Turkmenistan) and India. Since October 2001, the Euro-Atlantic community has the basic ability to influence directly the situation in Afghanistan. However, the war continues throughout Afghanistan and the coalition forces have been unable to secure peace in the country. It is obvious that it is impossible to establish peace in Afghanistan through military means. Its prolonged execution resulted in only one consequence—the conflict in the region has become wider, deeper and sharper.

The Central Asian states of Tajikistan, Turkmenistan and Uzbekistan have common borders with Afghanistan. For safeguarding the interests of the three neighbouring Central Asian countries, it is essential that Afghanistan is stabilised and demilitarised. India is also deeply interested in the stabilisation of Afghanistan. The shortest route from the Indian subcontinent to Central Asia passes through Pakistan and Afghanistan. The big challenge for India and the new states of Central Asia is to establish direct trade and transport corridors.

The 7+5 Formula for Afghanistan

Obviously, for peaceful settlement of Afghan problem, it is necessary to have direct participation of the states bordering this country, as well as key actors in the region. Thus, a liaison group may be formed under the formula 7+5, which implies first of all participation of seven states having a common border with Afghanistan—Tajikistan, China, India, Pakistan, Iran, Turkmenistan and Uzbekistan, along with the participation of Russia, USA, NATO, SCO and CSTO. However, this form of cooperation can be complicated by confrontation of Iran and the United States and the lack of cooperation of two countries. However, recently in the history of two states there has been a precedent of cooperation that gave positive results. Thus, following September 11, 2001 Iran supported the USA in the overthrow of Taliban power and elimination of the network of 'Al-Qaeda' in Afghan territory. Iran provided intelligence data on whereabouts of the 'Taliban' and 'Al-Qaeda'.[6]

Many neighbouring countries of Afghanistan happen to be members of Collective Security Treaty Organisation (CSTO) and constitute the zone of the latter's responsibility. This creates the necessity of NATO-CSTO cooperation for stabilising Afghanistan. However, the prospects of NATO-CSTO cooperation are complicated by many unresolved issues between the two organisations, and above all, by the reluctance of NATO to accept CSTO in the area of its responsibility.

The possibility of using the platform of SCO for promoting the convergence of positions and reduction of tension in international relations may also be considered. In March 2009, the SCO organised a conference on Afghanistan, which—for the first time in the history of the organisation, was attended by NATO, United States, and other states of the 'Group of Eight', Turkey and OSCE.

In the region of 'the Afghan problem', eight international organisations are involved. The activity of each of them is limited to its own plans, without coordination of efforts with potential partners from other countries. The need of the hour is joining of hands by the international community and concerned international organisations.

As is known, in 2008 the U.S. administration of Barack Obama has developed a new formula to combat international terrorism in Central Asia entitled 'Af-Pak' (Afghanistan-Pakistan), whose main purpose is to unite all the potential forces (social, economic, human, diplomatic, military, etc.) of both the countries in the fight against Islamic extremism and international terrorism. What is happening in this region has strong relation to the security of member countries and observer countries of SCO. India is also interested in the peace and stability of the region as it directly impacts on India's security.

Stability in Afghanistan can be achieved only through negotiations and finding compromises, as well as by promotion of economic development of the country. Tajik expert Kh. Kholiqnazarov also believes that for an Afghan settlement the United States should actively involve the neighbouring countries of Afghanistan, such as India, China, Iran, and neighbouring CIS countries in the negotiating process to resolve the Afghan conflict.

At the same time, the political struggle in Afghanistan is inseparable from the regional, as well as from inter-ethnic and inter-confessional (Sunni and Shia) contradictions.[7] The existing geopolitical realities within Afghanistan should not be ignored. The centralised power of Kabul is fairly weak and there is actual decentralisation in Afghanistan. Organisation of intra-Afghan dialogue could be based on the precedent of the policy of national reconciliation followed in the country in the second half of 1980. The experience of inter-Tajik settlement in 1997 with the participation of Iran and Russia could also be relevant for Afghanistan. Perhaps for good governance it is necessary to create autonomous regions in Afghanistan, and to give Afghanistan itself the status of a neutral state.

Partnership for Peace and Development

Central Asian states are broadly interested in creating a strong and independent Afghanistan. As regards Tajikistan, it is now seriously interested in cooperating with Afghanistan economically. Tajikistan is planning to implement a number of projects that can contribute to the development of Afghanistan. For example, the implementation of the proposed construction of railway link between Turkmenistan-Afghanistan (Mazar-i-Sharif)-Tajikistan; the gas pipeline along this route; as well as accelerated construction of energy project power transmission line (PTL) CASA-1000 (Central Asia-South Asia), which would connect the electric networks of Kyrgyzstan, Tajikistan, Afghanistan and Pakistan. These projects can significantly contribute to the development of northern Afghanistan, and promote regional cooperation and security. In addition, the project of possible construction of a railway through the Wakhan corridor may provide an alternative transport and communication link and restore the geopolitical integrity of Central Asia. Such a project could link the states such as Tajikistan, Afghanistan, Pakistan, India and China. Perhaps this project could be discussed and implemented within the bounds of SCO.

It seems that for India, the SCO platform is important for implementation of their national interests in Central Asian region. For the fast-growing economy of India the states in the region have a great market for industrial products, a prospective source of resources and the transit corridor. Perspective for India in the SCO framework is the realisation of the project Euro-Asian railway Tajikistan-Uzbekistan-Afghanistan-Pakistan-India. The agreement on its construction was achieved in 50's of the 20th century by the governments of the USSR, India and Afghanistan. Then this project was as follows: Termez-Mazar-e-Sharif-Kabul-Jalalabad-Peshawar-Islamabad-New Delhi.

At present, in connection with the implementation of large-scale communications projects by Tajikistan, Tajik railways can be included in this project. Moreover, the Member States of the South Asian Association for Regional Cooperation (SAARC), with Afghanistan as its member—have also underscored the necessity of establishing a through railway communication within the scope of the bloc. Perhaps, exactly within the scope of SCO the Indian initiative of the Asian oil and gas networks, which may connect India, Bangladesh, Iran, China, Korea, Myanmar, Pakistan, Afghanistan, Russia, Thailand, Japan and the new states of Central Asia can be implemented. The implementation of communication and energy projects can be a point of contact at the initial stage of interaction between SAARC and the SCO.

The Central Asian States clearly recognise that to realise their interests there should be the internal stability of Afghanistan. Afghanistan, as an observer in the SCO is in the zone of responsibility of the organisation. In this context it is interesting proposal of the Russian 'expert group of U. Krupnov' to establish an Afghan fund of SCO on developing and implementing a comprehensive plan of development of Afghanistan.[8] SCO may become the initiator and guarantor of the intra-regional negotiation process.

In case of another scenario, the Afghan conflict may become more protracted. The USA and EU, while reducing the International Security Assistance Force in Afghanistan de jure beginning with July 2011, may remain in the country de facto with the international projects, the financial impact and management. It is most likely that a new phase of rivalry may start between the participants in international relations in Central Asia. In this political process, the stabilising role of India is enormous, considering its place and role in world politics.

NOTES

1. Komissina I., "*Stanet li India polnopravnym uchastnikom 'Bolshoi igry' v Tsentralnoi Azii?*" *Tsentralnaya Azia I Kavkaz* (Sweden), Vol. 55, No. 1, 2008, pp. 68-69.
2. Nasretdinov, S.A., "*Ugrozy, vyzovy i riski v regione Srednevo Vostoka posle 22 dekabrya 1991 goda i 11 sentyabrya 2001 goda*" in *Materialy mezhdunarodnoi konferentsi "Srednii Vostok v sisteme geopoliticheskikh koordinat: proshloe, nastoyashee, budushee"*, Dushanbe, 2005, p. 6; Maytdinova, G.M., "*Osnovnye ugrozy i vyzovy v geopoliticheskom prostranstve Tsentralnoi Azii i problema obespecheniya bezopasnosti*", *Problema bezopasnosti v geopoliticheskom komplekse Tsentralnoi Azii,* Dushanbe, 2004, pp. 32-33.
3. Maytdinova G., "Geopolitika Tsentr. Azii, formiruetsya novaya podsistema mezhdunarodnykh otnoshenii", geopolitica.ru http://www.centrasia.ru/newsA.php?st=1268213880.
4. Pilko A., "Tsentralnoi Azii grozit 'Afghanizatsia' ", *Russia Profile at* Zpress.kg, http://www.centrasia.ru/newsA.php?st=1278828780.
5. *Otchyot o rabote mezhdunarodnoi konferensii "Afghanistan, SHOS, bezopasnost i geopolitika Tsentralnoi Evrazii"* Issyk-Kul, June 10-12, 2008, Bishkek, 2008, p. 11.
6. Stolpovskii O.A., *"Potentsial vliyaniya Irana na razvitie situatsii v Afghanistane"*, in *Materialy mezhdunarodnoi konferentsii "SHOS kak factor integratsii Tsentralnoi Evrazii: potentsial stran-nablyudatelei i stran-sosedei"*, M., 2009, p.124.
7. Knyazev A.A., "*Amerikanskii tupik v Afghanistane, SHOS i znachenie stran-nablyudatelei: poisk novykh paradigm," materialy mezhdunarodnoi konferentsii "SHOS kak factor integratsii Tsentralnoi Evrazii: potensial stran-nablyudatelei i stran-sosedei"*, M., 2009, p. 135.
8. *Путь к миру и согласию в Афганистане определяется позицией, которую займет Россия.* Проектно-аналитический доклад. М.,2008.

6

Prospects of Mutual Relations of the Republic of Tajikistan with India

Khaibatullo Shodiev

The Republic of Tajikistan from the moment of gaining independence has actively joined the policy and norms of the world community and has directed its efforts towards pursuing an 'open doors' policy with all the states of the world community. Tajikistan has achieved the image of a reliable partner among far and near countries as a result of following this widely accepted policy.

During the period of the united Soviet Union also, mutual relations of the Republic of Tajikistan and the Republic of India had been established at a good level—through exhibitions including that of books. There were celebrations of the days of each other's culture. Students from the departments of Urdu and Hindi languages of the faculty of Oriental languages of Tajik State University passed their training in India and other academic and cultural exchanges took place from time to time.

Following the independence of the Republic of Tajikistan in September 1991, a new stage of the country's bilateral ties with countries of the world community, including with the Republic of India began.

India was one of the first countries to recognise the independence of the Republic of Tajikistan. The agreement to establish diplomatic relations between the two was signed on August 28, 1992. The Indian Embassy in Dushanbe has been functioning since May 1994. On June 11 1993, the President of Tajikistan issued decree No. 1098 whereby it was decided to open the Tajik diplomatic mission in India. Tajikistan opened its diplomatic mission in India in August 1994. On August 28, 2007, the two countries observed 15 years of the establishment of diplomatic relations.[1] Tajik trade representation in the Republic of India was opened in September 1997 for the development of trade and economic relations between the two countries. The relations between the two countries are characterised by close political contacts, interaction on the widest spectrum of questions and coincidence of positions of the parties on important regional and international problems.

Tajikistan occupies a strategically important position in Central Asia, on the border with Afghanistan and China and is separated from Pakistan by a small strip of Afghan territory—Wakhan corridor. World powers give much importance to Tajikistan's position. India is one of the successfully developing countries among the world community, whose priority interests truly coincide with the strategic interests of the Republic of Tajikistan. In the new changing geopolitical scenario, New Delhi's authorities recognise Tajikistan as the important strategic partner in Central Asia. Tajikistan has historical links with India and it promotes mutual and priority interests of the two countries.

In the development of the Tajik-Indian relations, the mutual visits of the state delegations of the Republic of Tajikistan and India in the period between 1993-2010 played an important role. During these visits they signed a number of agreements, which laid down a strong contractual-legal basis for the development and strengthening of cooperation between the two countries in various areas of economy, science and culture.

The basic documents of the economic character are:

- The agreement on trade and economic cooperation, including cooperation in the field of industry;

- The agreement on the inter-governmental commission on trade, economic, scientific and technical cooperation;
- The agreement on encouragement and protection of investments.

Tajikistan and India have a solid base for the development of relations in such areas as power, mining, light industry, construction, tourism and other such areas.

The intergovernmental commission on trade, economic, scientific and technical cooperation has been formed to encourage trade and investment in hydropower, energy, transport, extraction of minerals, food processing, construction and tourism. India has also helped in reconstruction and the modernisation of the Varzob-I Hydropower Plant.

For implementation of the agreement on encouragement of investments, groups of businessmen from India visited Tajikistan. As a result, a number of concrete contracts were signed. These include, the construction of a hotel and factory of mineral water in Penjikent, reconstruction of the wine factory and establishment of the joint venture 'Kokhe Amir Khusrau' in Uratube and the opening of a trading house in Khojend. Agreement has also been reached about the construction of a five-star hotel in the capital Dushanbe.

Presently, several Tajik-Indian joint ventures have been registered, such as: 'Karmel Overseas Ltd.', 'Tajik Metals and Minerals', 'Gulf-Tour' and 'Shabakai Osmoni'.

In November, 2003, the Prime Minister of India, Atal Bihari Vajpayee paid an official visit to the Republic of Tajikistan. During the visit, a number of the documents, strengthening the normative-legal base of the mutual relations were signed, including: the Memorandum between the Governments of the Republic of Tajikistan and the Republic of India about setting up of the Tajik-Indian Information Technology (IT) Centre; the Memorandum between the Tajik Ministry of Economy and Trade and Indian Ministry of Communications and Information Technologies of the Republic of

India about the cooperation in the field of information technologies and services.

The Tajik President Emomali Rahmon visited India from August 6-10, 2006. During the visit, the official signing ceremony of the following five bilateral documents was held:

1. The joint declaration of the Republic of Tajikistan and the Republic of India on the further development of friendship and cooperation;
2. The memorandum of mutual understanding in the field of consultations between Foreign Ministries of the Republic of Tajikistan and the Republic of India;
3. The memorandum of mutual understanding between the Governments of the Republic of Tajikistan and of the Republic of India in the field of energy;
4. The cooperation programme between the Governments of the Republic of Tajikistan and of the Republic of India in the field of culture and art for 2006-2008;
5. The cooperation programme between the Tajik Academy of Sciences and Indian Department of Science and Technology for 2006-2008.

In September 2009 the President of India, Pratibha Devisingh Patil made an official visit to Tajikistan and participated in the country's Independence Day celebrations. During this visit a number of documents promoting further development and strengthening of relations between the Republic of Tajikistan and Republic of India were signed.

The Indian President supported the initiatives of the Tajik President and the Government on development of the regional cooperation in the field of hydro-power engineering, creation of the regional market of electric power, implementation of projects in the sphere of transport and road building, and also on assistance in the economic restoration of Afghanistan. In its turn, Tajikistan supported the India's aspiration to become a permanent member of the U.N. Security Council.

At present, one of the priorities between Tajikistan and India is cooperation in the sphere of education. Cooperation in this field is regulated by the cooperation agreement between the Governments of the Republic of Tajikistan and the Republic of India in the areas of culture, art, education, mass-media and sports signed on December 12, 1995. At present, 334 Indian nationals are studying in Tajik institutions of higher learning.

Under the Indian Technical and Economic Cooperation (ITEC) programme, Tajik government officials are getting professional training in various institutions in India. In 1993, the Government of India allocated 20 seats annually for Tajikistan under this programme. The number was subsequently raised to 50 and since 2009, this number was further raised to 70 per annum. At present India provides 100 slots annually to Tajik professionals for training in India in various short-term courses.

India assisted Tajikistan in the reconstruction of the military airfield 'Ayni'. India provides professional training for the armed forces of Tajikistan in Indian military schools and also helps in improvement of the material-technical base of Tajik Army. For the improvement of the combat training of Tajik armed forces, joint exercises of military units of the two countries are held. Also for the maintenance of security, contacts are maintained on a regular basis within the framework of the working group on struggle against terrorism and religious extremism.

By way of conclusion, it may be said that the Tajik-Indian relations have a great potential for development and the parties are full of determination to realise it practically.

NOTES

1. http://www.tajikembassy.in/html/tajik_india_relation.html

7

India-Tajikistan Relations: Prospects for Cooperation

Meena Singh Roy

Today Tajikistan's strategic location has made it an important area of big power rivalry and competition. Post-2001 it has become a playground for major powers-Russia, U.S. and China. Russia has a military base and continues to enhance its engagement with Dushanbe giving it a strong foothold in Tajikistan. The U.S. enhanced its engagement with Tajikistan after 9/11 as it offered three military facilities to the U.S. Air Force to carry out its offensive operation against the Taliban. Since then many high level visits have taken place and Washington has also increased its military contacts with Tajikistan. In the current context, Tajikistan's role in Afghanistan is critical for the U.S. and NATO forces that are fighting Taliban. Its strategic relevance for the U.S. is immense.

China has been increasing its profile through economic, energy and military engagement with Tajikistan. It has provided a preferential loan under the SCO framework in 2006. This loan was used mainly in infrastructure and road construction. In total, China has invested around U.S. $1billion since 2005. China is also the main partner of

Tajikistan in developing the hydropower sector. There are plans to build several hydro and thermal power plants with Chinese participation. Some 80 Chinese companies have been recorded as operating in Tajikistan in 2008.

Tajikistan's importance for India lies in its geo-strategic location. Tajikistan is physically the closest to the Indian subcontinent. It shares a border with Uzbekistan, Kyrgyzstan, Afghanistan, and China and is located in proximity to PoK.[1] All these countries are of great strategic importance to India. In India's regional security calculus, Tajikistan assumes a significant place, especially in the context of Afghanistan and Pakistan. Tajikistan can play an important role in maintaining peace along Afghanistan's northern borders and fighting 'jihadis' and drug traffickers.[2] The infiltration of extremist forces in Tajikistan can have serious security implication for India because of its proximity to PoK and likely proliferation of this problem into Kashmir.

In addition to its strategic location, Tajikistan has deposits of more than 40 semi-precious stones, gold and silver. It also has hydroelectric power. It has the largest natural water resources in the region. It has more than 65 percent of the glaciers in the region. In fact, 90 percent of the water resources of Central Asia are with Kyrgyzstan and Tajikistan. There are large reserves of mercury, brown coal, lead, zinc, antimony and tungsten, and unpublicised uranium deposits.[3] These resources make Tajikistan a significantly important country in the region that offers many opportunities to India.

This paper is an attempt to analyse various dimensions of India-Tajikistan relations since 1991 and examines future areas of cooperation between India and Tajikistan. It argues that in the context of recent developments in the South and Central Asian region there is need to embark on a multidimensional new approach to ensure mutually beneficial relationship between the two countries.

Political Ties

India and Tajikistan have maintained the tradition of close political understanding and mutual cooperation. During Tajikistan's civil war period, India continued to be in touch with the countries of the region and offered its help in finding solution to the problem. Since the visit of Tajik Prime Minister, Abdumalik Abdullojanov in February 1993 and with the establishment of the resident Indian Mission in Tajik capital Dushanbe contacts between the two countries have increased significantly.[4] These ties were considerably strengthened by the visits of President of Tajikistan, Emomali Rahmon to Delhi during December 1995 and January 1999. During the 1995 visit, President of Tajikistan and Prime Minister of India signed a declaration on further development of bilateral relations. Agreements were signed on setting up of the Indo-Tajik Joint Commission, cooperation on environment, health, telecom, science and technology, and on bilateral investment protection.[5] In 1996, India also provided a loan of $5 million which was seen by Tajiks as a significant aid during the country's difficult conditions of civil war.[6]

In 1997, eight slots were offered for short-term training courses to Tajikistan under the ITEC programme and three scholarships under the aegis of the Indian Council for Cultural Relations (ICCR).[7]

During President Rahmon's visit to India in May 2001, Indo-Tajik ties were further strengthened. Five agreements including one on economic cooperation and another for joint action against terrorism and drug trafficking were signed. This agreement included a treaty for legal assistance in criminal matters as well. In addition, a memorandum of understanding (MoU) was concluded on technical cooperation including an agreement on air services. India also offered a grant of $ 5 million as assistance toward drought relief in Tajikistan. The Indian Prime Minister also announced the gift of a fruit-processing plant to Tajikistan. During his visit the Tajik leader fully supported India's aspiration to join an expanded U.N. Security Council.[8] The Minister of State for External Affairs, Omar Abdullah, visited Tajikistan in September 2001 and handed over a gift of anti-tuberculosis medicines worth Rs.20 lakhs.

The proposal of setting up of a fruit-processing plant by HMT (international) and implementation of humanitarian assistance to Tajikistan announced by Prime Minister were also reviewed. Ten slots under the ITEC programme were allotted to Tajikistan. The first meeting of the Indo-Tajik Joint Commission was held in December 2001 where new areas for cooperation, including areas such as industry, tourism, civil aviation, training and exchanges of business delegates were identified.[9]

During the Tajik President's visit to New Delhi in May 2003 joint declaration on principles of mutual relations, five agreements including one on combating drug trafficking and another for enhanced economic cooperation were signed to give thrust to the bilateral relations. A MoU on technical cooperation and air services agreement was also signed.[10] In January 2003, a protocol on cooperation in the fight against international terrorism and agreement on providing Indian assistance to Tajikistan in the construction of an agriculture goods processing plant were signed during the External Affairs Minister's visit.[11] India has also been providing aid to Tajikistan during crisis situation. In December 2002 India supplied over 10,000 tonnes of food to Tajikistan, in areas stricken by natural calamities.[12]

Prime Minister Atal Bihari Vajpayee's two-day visit in November 2003 was a landmark in enhancing Indo-Tajik cooperation. Documents signed during this trip included technology exchange, tourism and visa-free travel for diplomats. A declaration on friendship and cooperation was also signed. There was also an agreement on establishing direct air links between Dushanbe and New Delhi, opening up of the Tajik mission in Delhi, and forming of a working group(represented by Afghanistan, India and Tajikistan) on a direct land route between two countries via Afghanistan. The desire to extend the New Delhi-Dushanbe air route to Kabul was expressed by Indian Prime Minister. The main theme of this meeting was the importance of developing regional transport infrastructure to improve Tajikistan's economic outlook. On the eve of this visit the Tajik parliament endorsed a resolution to join the 1997 Treaty on International Transit of Goods, a tripartite agreement between India, Iran, and Turkmenistan. The treaty aims to facilitate trade cooperation by eliminating various import duties and custom procedures.

The most significant outcome of this meeting, however, was an agreement to create a Joint Working Group (JWG) on Counter

Terrorism. Both countries underlined the purpose of this group, "will be to contribute to the battle and resistance against organised crime, money laundering, illegal trade in weapons, military supplies, and explosives, the war against international terrorism and other forces of international threats."[13] The JWG held its first meeting in Dushanbe in January 2006. During this meeting, a protocol was signed on mutual assistance to combat criminal activities. The second meeting was held in August 2006 in Delhi.[14]

President Emomali S. Rahmon's visit in August 2006 has further strengthened the Indo-Tajik ties. During this visit five documents on energy, trade, security, science and technology and culture were inked. Under these agreements there is an active cooperation going on between Indian Biologists and Geneticists and Institute of Plant Physiology of Academy of Sciences of Tajikistan.[15] In response to the appeal of President Rahmon for humanitarian aid to overcome the crisis due to harsh winter and shortages of power in Tajikistan during January-February 2008, Indian Prime Minister announced a grant of US $ 2 million of which $1million was provided as cash assistance and the remaining one million as goods consisting of power cables, generators and pump sets. Again in 2009, US$200,000 cash assistance was granted by India to overcome the damages caused by floods in Tajikistan during April-May 2009.[16]

India-Tajikistan relations got a further impetus during President Rahmon's fifth visit to India from September 1-4, 2012. Six important agreements in the field of culture, education, sports, textile, social and labour relations and cooperation in health and medicine were inked.[17] India also offered to undertake a series of new development projects in Tajikistan. These include: an IT centre, medical centres, language labs, supply of agriculture machinery and the implementation of a package of small development projects as well as setting up of a fruit and vegetable processing plant. Both sides also agreed to enhance cooperation in hydel power, solar and other forms of renewable energy and to start discussion on regional energy infrastructure network. One of the major development projects agreed upon by India is setting up of the India-Tajik Friendship Hospital in Tajikistan. This is a further boost to India's increasing strategic partnership with Tajikistan under the framework of newly announced 'connect Central Asia' Policy.[18]

Tajikistan is one of the largest beneficiaries of Indian Technical and Economic Cooperation (ITEC) programme. Over the years India has provided training and participation for candidates from Tajikistan in number of human resource development programmes in various fields. By the end of the 2009, 518 slots for ITEC and 212 ICCR scholarships had been utilised by Tajik candidates to study in India. After the visit of India's President in 2009 the number of ITEC slots for Tajikistan was increased from 70 to 100. During President Rahmon's visit in September1-4, 2012 the number of ITEC slots were further increased to 150.[19] India announced a grant to setup an "India-Tajikistan Modern Engineering Workshop" at the Tajik State Technical University (TTU) in Dushanbe which was inaugurated on June 2, 2011.[20]

The three day visit of President Pratibha Patil to Tajikistan from September 6 to 8, 2009 was the first ever visit by a President of India to the Central Asian region. She attended the National Day celebrations of Tajikistan as Guest of Honour. During this visit the President held talks with Tajik President Emomali Rahmon on a wide range of issues including efforts to tackle terrorism, bilateral relations, and developments in and around the region aimed at consolidating ties between the two countries in political, economic and other spheres. President Patil also held meetings with the Prime Minister, the Foreign Minister, and the Defence Minister of Tajikistan and interacted with the Chairman and Members of the Lower House of the Tajik Parliament.[21]

Although no bilateral official documents were signed during this visit but the significance of this visit lies in India's effort in placing Tajikistan on a high prism of New Delhi's radar screen. This visit is also indicative of Tajikistan's critical importance for India and about enhancing goodwill, trust and confidence between the two countries. India's increasing focus and importance of this region in its overall policy was stated by President Patil during her visit to Tajikistan in 2009. She stated, "The Central Asian region figures very high in our foreign policy priorities. We would like our bilateral relations with

Tajikistan to be truly multi-faceted and cover wide ranging areas from cooperation in the field of education and culture to investment and enhanced business transactions. We would like our bilateral relations to address the contemporary and crucial issues of energy, food and regional security." Both India and Tajikistan face common threats and challenges in the region. The commonalty of interest provides greater opportunity to both India and Tajikistan to cooperate more closely in addressing the regional security issues of extremism and terrorism.

Terrorism and Extremism

Terrorism and extremism constitute a common threat faced by India and Tajikistan. In the past, both countries along with Russia and Iran have worked together in the fight against the Taliban. There is already a Joint Working Group on Counter Terrorism between India and Tajikistan. In 2006 during President Emomali Rahmon's visit to India four bilateral pacts were signed to fight global terrorism and enhance cooperation in the field of science, technology and energy.

Terrorism was an important issue discussed during the 2009 visit of President Patil. Speaking on this issue she sought the Central Asian nations support in eliminating terrorism from the region. She said, "Our region is today beset by the menace of terrorism. Terrorism, extremism and fundamentalism are posing a serious threat to the peace and security in our region, be it India, Afghanistan or Tajikistan."[22] While referring to the Mumbai attacks as one more manifestation of terrorism, she pointed out that all governments of the region needed to take "urgent proactive measures to cooperate and eliminate terrorism in all its forms and manifestations, so that these forces do not derail the processes of progress and prosperity."[23]

In the context of increasing violence in Pakistan, re-emergence of Taliban in Afghanistan and the proposed withdrawal of U.S. forces in 2014, cooperation between India and Tajikistan once again require urgent attention by policy makers on both sides. These developments are likely to have serious security implications for both India and Tajikistan. Extremist activities have been on the rise in Tajikistan in the past year. Stability and peace in Tajikistan and Afghanistan are equally important for India. Cooperation in the security arena needs to be intensified not only at bilateral level but enhanced at the regional level too. Increasingly disturbing developments in the Afghanistan-Pakistan region clubbed with the future scenario of U.S. withdrawal in 2014 from Afghanistan are of great concern to both the countries. During President Rahmon's recent visit to India in September 2012, continued cooperation in the field of fighting terrorism and extremism has been agreed between the two sides.

Hydroelectric Power

Tajikistan has immense potential for hydroelectric power. The country is the second largest producer of hydroelectricity in the CIS after Russia. Its potential according to official figures is about 40,000MW that is around four percent of the world's hydroelectric potential. According to the official report 'Tajikistan's National Strategy for Energy Sector Development 2006-2015', the country was likely to reach a production of 26 billion Kwh in 2010, and 35 billion in 2015. However, what is important to note here is that despite this potential Tajikistan produces only 17 billion Kwh per year and has to import energy from Uzbekistan. The country needs investment in this sector. Russia, Iran and China are involved in Tajikistan. India is providing help in Varzob-I Hydro-Power Station. Hydroelectric power was another important issue discussed during President Pratibha Patil's visit in 2009. The progress of Varzob-I Hydro-Power Station upgraded by Indian companies National Hydro Power Corporation (NHPC) and BHEL was reviewed. India's involvement in this sector needs to be enhanced as this will be mutually beneficial for both the countries.

Cultural Cooperation

In addition, India and Tajikistan have a number of commonalties that make a closer relationship likely. Close historical and civilisation ties between the two countries play an important role in bringing the people of both countries together. Cultural similarities have enabled both countries to maintain close cooperation in culture with regular exchanges of cultural troupes. Indian movies and songs are very popular in Tajikistan. The Indian Cultural Centre (ICC) inaugurated in 2003 by then External Affairs Minister Yashwant Sinha in the Indian Embassy has been very active. Hindi classes are conducted in ICC and so far 620 students have been trained in both beginners and advanced level Hindi courses. More importantly, cultural and literary connections between the people of India and Tajikistan going back to 16th and 17th century have played a major role in bringing two countries closer. A famous Tajik poet Mirzo Tursunzade wrote many poems after his visit to India which were published under the title 'Indian Ballad'. The works of Rabindranath Tagore and Premchand are very popular in Tajikistan. Similarly, the works of famous Tajik writer Sadriddin Aini are appreciated and popular among the Indian readers.

Central Asia has been the meeting point for traders, travellers and mercantile communities from India, Iran, China and Europe.[24] Many scholars, travellers, historians, poets and geographers have travelled across from Central Asia to India. Some of important names like: Ibn Battuta, Al-Beruni, Sharafuddin Yazdi, Mirza Haidar Dughlat and Abul Fazal are indicative of close cultural cooperation which flourished through the Silk Route in past. India was linked to Central Asia through Kashmir with Sogdiana (part of Tajikistan and Afghanistan), Andijon, Tashkent, Badakhshon, Bactria (Balakh/Afghanistan), Gandhara (Peshawar) and China across the Pamir, Hindukush, Karakorum and the Tie'n Shan mountains.[25] These long standing historical and cultural ties provide a very strong base for future cooperation in the area of education and culture between India and Tajikistan. These ties need to be reinvigorated.

President Patil's visit in 2009 to the Mausoleum of the Sufi Saint Sayyid Ali Hamadani in Kulyab was yet another step towards strengthening the close historical and civilisation links between Tajikistan and Kashmir. The Iranian Sufi Saint Hamadani moved to Kashmir in 1314 with 700 of his followers and during his stay had greatly influenced the religious, social and cultural aspects of Kashmiri society. The Shah-e-Hamadan mosque in Srinagar attracts thousands of people even today to congregate at Saint's death anniversary.

Economic and Trade Cooperation

To analyse economic relations between India and Tajikistan it is important to examine the overall economic ties between India and other Central Asian countries as well. Trade and economic relations between India and CARs stay the most unsatisfactory aspect of an otherwise potentially beneficial relationship. India's trade relations with all CARs are conducted under the framework of Inter-Governmental Commission on Trade, Economic, Scientific and Technological Cooperation. The ground situation portrays a very low level of trade when compared with India's overall trade with other countries, limited number of joint ventures and no worthwhile investment in Central Asia by Indian business and industry, though there are small government credit lines. While trade between the India and CARs has been increasing (see Fig. 1 and Table 1) but CARs do not even figure any where among India's top 25 trading partners (See Table 2).This can be attributed to the poor connectivity with the region, lack of interest and motivation on the part of major Indian companies, and difficult local environment. If one looks at India's over all trade with Central Asian countries, Kazakhstan figures as the main trading partner of India. While Kazakhstan's total trade has increased from US$ 96.8million in 2004-5 to $154.45 million in 2009-2010, trade with Tajikistan has increased from $10.7 million in 2004-05 to $32.56 million only. The trade figures reflect a very low level of trade between India-and Tajikistan.

As compared to India's strong political and security ties its economic relations remain unsatisfactory. The dissatisfaction over the low level of trade between India and Tajikistan was expressed during President Patil's visit as well. Both the Presidents said that there was immense potential to enhance the cooperation in economic arena and take trade volume beyond the current level.

Indian investments in Tajikistan include a five star hotel being constructed by CHL Company, exploration of natural gas in south Tajikistan by Marvis Ltd. and three Indian restaurants in Dushanbe. The BHEL has supplied a 7 MW generator to Tajik company 'Pamir Energy' and this project too was completed in 2010.

Figure 1: Trade with Central Asian Countries (in US $ Million)

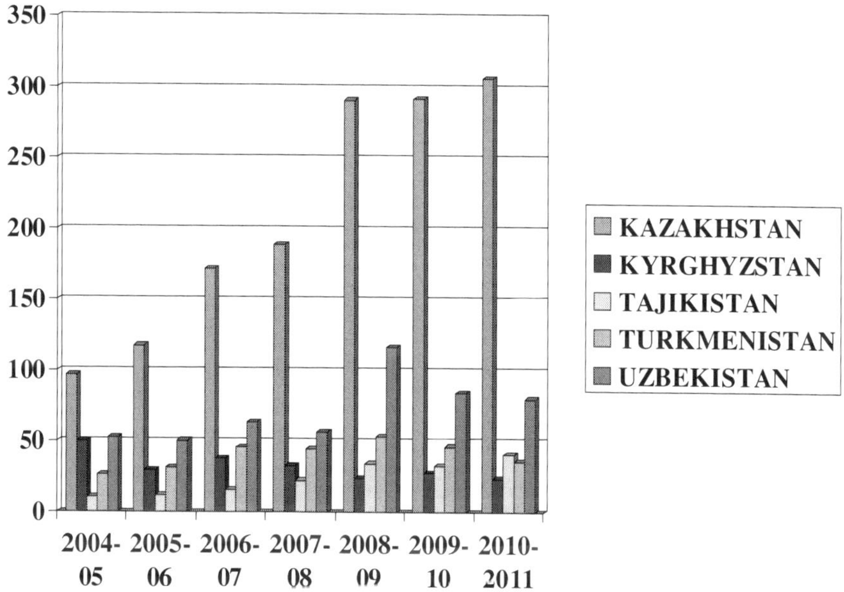

Source: Ministry of Commerce, India at http://commerce.nic.in/eidb/default.asp

There are a few representatives of Indian pharmaceutical companies working in Tajikistan and Indian businessmen have formed an Indian Business Advisory Group. The modernisation of the Varzob-1 Hydro Power Station (costing approx US$ 17 mn) through Indian companies BHEL and NHPC is expected to be completed at the end of 2012[26] Further boost to the economic cooperation between the two countries were provided during President Rahmon's visit in September 2012 when the MoU between Ministry of Energy and Industry of the Tajikistan and Ministry of Textiles of India was inked. This envisages enhancing trade and economic relations in the field of textiles, clothing and fashion. Research and development, investment cooperation and promoting export of textiles in each other's market are some important initiatives in this regard. Setting up of JWG on textiles will ensure the implementation of this MoU.

Table 1: Trade with Central Asian Republics, 2005-12
(US Million $)

Country	*2004-05*	*2005-06*	*2006-07*	*2007-08*	*2008-09*	*2009-10*	*2010-11*	*2011-12 (Apr-sep) 2012 (Apr-Sep)*
Kazakhstan	96.8	117	171.5	188.8	290.7	154.45	310.58	276.24
Kyrgyzstan	50.2	29.6	37.8	32.4	24.0	27.48	26.99	22.32
Tajikistan	10.7	12.1	15.4	22.2	34.20	32.56	41.33	17.72
Turkmenistan	26.1	31.2	45.9	44.7	53.5	46.15	35.89	45.24
Uzbekistan	52.8	50.6	63.6	56.5	116.3	83.98	81.05	107.79

Source: Ministry of Commerce, India at http://commerce.nic.in/eidb/default.asp

Table 2: Export Import Data Bank
Total Trade: Top 25 Countries

Dated: 11/09/2012
Values in US$ Million

Year: 2011-12 (Apr-Dec)

Rank	*Country*	*Export*	*Import*	*Total Trade*	*Trade Balance*
1.	China P RP	12,944.65	44,806.36	57,751.02	-31,861.71
2.	U Arab Emts	26,317.86	26,526.70	52,844.57	-208.84
3.	USA	25,326.88	17,900.94	43,227.82	7,425.94
4.	Saudi Arab	3,940.20	23,047.65	26,987.85	-19,107.45
5.	Switzerland	783.42	23,622.39	24,405.80	-22,838.97
6.	Singapore	12,686.77	6,577.55	19,264.31	6,109.22
7.	Hong Kong	9,350.88	8,718.65	18,069.53	632.24
8.	Germany	5,974.67	11,839.69	17,814.36	-5,865.01
9.	Indonesia	4,441.33	11,325.52	15,766.85	-6,884.18
10.	Unspecified	14,728.85	850.26	15,579.11	13,878.60
11.	Iraq	522.60	14,026.08	14,548.68	-13,503.49
12.	Japan	4,140.44	8,947.54	13,087.98	-4,807.10
13.	Belgium	5,333.32	7,736.38	13,069.70	-2,403.06
14.	Korea Rp	3,343.23	9,508.31	12,851.54	-6,165.07
15.	Nigeria	1,967.09	10,842.65	12,809.74	-8,875.56
16.	Australia	1,642.13	11,093.94	12,736.07	-9,451.80
17.	UK	6,484.72	5,998.53	12,483.25	486.20
18.	Kuwait	898.94	11,137.40	12,036.35	-10,238.46
19.	South Africa	3,479.19	7,640.19	11,119.38	-4,161.00
20.	Iran	1,904.59	8,593.94	10,498.53	-6,689.34
21.	Malaysia	2,837.46	7,131.68	9,969.14	-4,294.22
22.	Qatar	608.42	9,291.43	9,899.85	-8,683.01
23.	Netherland	7,171.28	1,771.25	8,942.52	5,400.03
24.	Italy	3,704.09	4,160.23	7,864.32	-456.14
25.	Brazil	4,173.30	2,768.67	6,941.97	1,404.63
	Total of Top 25 countries	164,706.34	295,863.90	460,570.24	-131,157.57
	India's Total	226,192.38	361,818.79	588,001.02	-135,626.41

Source: Ministry of Commerce India at http://commerce.nic.in/eidb/iecnttopn.asp (accessed on September 5,2012)

The existing economic engagement between India and Central Asia in general and Tajikistan in particular is quite disappointing. Nevertheless, potential for comparative economic advantages for the two regions is vast only if long term policy towards this region is formulated. Central Asia provides a sizable consumer market for a range of goods and services, which India can provide. Both have economic complementarity in terms of resources, manpower and markets. For India, economic cooperation is possible through joint ventures in banking, insurance, agriculture, information technology, and the pharmaceutical industry. The construction sector has huge potential for India in Central Asia.While terrorism remains the major issue of cooperation, the CARs are looking for Indian involvement in the information technology (IT) sector and using India's experience in setting up various industrial units related to agriculture and defence, providing training in financial and banking sectors, and helping build their national economy through scientific and technological cooperation. India could be a principal driver in establishing cooperation among these states.[27]

Defence Cooperation

Economic and commercial linkages provide the best instrumentality for forging closer ties with any region. However, defence engagement can be utilised as an effective foreign policy tool. Some analysts are of the view that despite India's wide-ranging approach to international defence and military cooperation, "foreign military relations, in the form of international defence and military cooperation, have never been a serious tool of its foreign policy"[28] The Group of Ministers' Report of 2001 does highlight this aspect. However, there are no recommendations to suggest the use of defence and military cooperation to be used as a foreign policy tool.[29] To optimise the benefit from the defence engagement with foreign countries, it is important that defence cooperation policy is aligned with the government's foreign policy and security objectives. In fact, defence and diplomacy are the two sides of the same coin. Given the current level of India's defence engagement with CARs, there is a need to intensify this cooperation. India's benign image, growing economy and technological strength offer it a great opportunity to engage these countries in some specific sectors. Keeping in view India's long term interests in Central Asian region, it is important that defence engagement with this region should form the priority of its policy towards the Central Asian region.

While India's political relations with CARs have been growing, its cooperation in defence still remain low. The details shown in Table-3 and 4 clearly indicate that much needs to be done in terms of increasing defence and security cooperation with CARs. As compared to Turkmenistan and Kyrgyzstan, India's defence engagement is more with Tajikistan, Uzbekistan and Kazakhstan in that order. Though the process of defence cooperation with CARs was initiated much before 2001, it gained momentum only after 2001. The main features of the recent defence and security cooperation are:

- Intelligence sharing
- Providing training and assistance
- Military and technical cooperation
- Servicing and upgrading military hardware
- Joint military exercise (Tajikistan)
- Manufacturing transport aircraft with Uzbekistan (IL-78 air-to-air refuellers.)
- Acquiring of torpedoes from Kazakhstan
- Providing helicopters (2) to Kazakhstan
- Joint working group on counter-terrorism

Table 3: Overview of India's Defence and Military Cooperation with CARs, Part-I

Country	*Formal Defence Agreement*	*Formal Defence Cooperation Agreement*	*Security Dialogue*	*Active Annual Cooperation Plans*	*Military Courses*
Kazakhstan	No	Yes	No	No	Yes in India
Kyrgyzstan	No	Yes	No	No	Yes in India
Tajikistan	Yes	Yes	No	Yes	Yes in India
Uzbekistan	No	Yes	No	Yes	Yes
Turkmenistan	No	No	No	No	No

Table 4: Overview of India's Defence and Military Cooperation with CARs, Part-II

Country	*Coop. Exch*	*Assistance*	*Defence Equipment*	*Visits*	*Military Exercise*
Kazakhstan	Yes	No	Import for India (torpedoes); India delivered 2 MI-8 in 2001	Yes	No
Kyrgyzstan	Yes	Co-developing torpedo testing center	Joint development	Yes	No
Tajikistan	Yes	Yes, help Building an air base	No	Yes	Yes

Table 5: Overview of India's Defence and Military Cooperation with CARs, Part-III

Country	*Coop. Exch*	*Assistance*	*Defence Equipment*	*Visits*	*Military Exercise*
Uzbekistan	Yes	No	Import for India Agreement on repairing Indian transport aircraft In Tashkent	Yes	No
Turkmenistan	No	No	No	Yes	No

Source: Colonel KA Muthanna, *Enabling Military-to-Military Cooperation as Foreign Policy Tool: Options for India*, Knowledge World, New Delhi, 2006, pp. 195-200; MOD Reports; Interaction with Indian and Central Asian Defence Attachés in Delhi on September 26-28, 2007. Military Balance, 2005-06, p. 255.

India and Tajikistan share close defence and security relations. India has upgraded the Ayni airport near Dushanbe,[30] which is fully operational now. There is an ongoing cooperation in the defence sector where India is providing training to Tajik forces and large number of Tajik military cadets and young officers also undergo training at various defence training institutes in India. This military training is offered free of charge to Tajik military personnel.

Indian Defence Minister George Fernandes led a high level military delegation to Dushanbe in April 2002 to discuss matters like training of Tajik defence personnel, service and possibly retrofit their military equipment, and teach English to Tajik army and air force personnel.[31] The Tajik armed forces are small with its total active armed forces being around 6,000.[32] But India and Tajikistan use similar equipments like T-72 tanks and BMP-II infantry combat vehicles. Therefore, possibility of retrofitting these equipments is very much there. There was also a Military Hospital run by India in Dushanbe which has been shifted to Afghanistan. In June 2002, a Defence Cooperation Agreement was signed with Tajikistan.[33] Given the strategic relevance of Tajikistan for India its defence and military cooperation needs to be further intensified.

Challenges and Future Prospects for Revitalising India-Tajikistan Relations

There is huge potential for close cooperation between India and Tajikistan but there are many challenges that limit the cooperation between India and Tajikistan. The biggest challenge in terms of developing Tajik-India economic and trade relations is the lack of adequate infrastructure connecting both countries. There are no roadways, railways or regular air connectivity with Tajikistan. Road connectivity between India and Tajikistan could be utilised only if Pakistan was willing to allow India to use the roads connecting Tajikistan. However, there does not seem to be any political will in Pakistan for this. It has also been pointed out by Tajik experts that 'Pakistan is not interested in the closeness of the Central Asian countries with India, since it considers these countries as a zone of its strategic interests'. The most effective route is Kurgan-tyube-Pyanj-Imam-Sahib-Kunduz-Baghlam-Salang Pass-Kabul, Jalalabad-Landi Kotal-Peshwar-Lahore and Amritsar.[34] However, none of this would be possible without the political will within Pakistan and more importantly stability in Afghanistan. Regional connectivity involving India, Pakistan, China, Afghanistan and Tajikistan can bring about stability and economic prosperity for the entire region.

In the changing regional situation, New Delhi will have to formulate a new policy approach to enhance its economic engagement with Tajikistan which remains geographically closer to New Delhi than some of its own cities. Both countries will have to jointly evolve new mechanisms—bilateral and regional—to address the problem areas. Given the reserves of precious stones, gold and silver which Tajikistan has, India can setup in cooperation with Tajikistan a jewellery complex with a network of branches in mountain areas of the country.[35] Such involvement will not only help India make its presence felt in a country of great significance but also contribute in the economy of Tajikistan.

The Indian private sector can be encouraged to invest in information technology, automobile sector, gold mining, chemical industry, food and light industry, machine building, construction and electrical manufacturing. There is huge potential in textile sector, processing of cotton, silk, leather and wool. Another promising area in Tajikistan is that of commercial farming, canning of fruits and vegetables, small-scale manufacturing units for producing non-alcoholic beverages and mineral water and packaging units for dried fruits. Tajik government provides its investors guarantee to repatriate profits and other amounts in foreign currency abroad. It has also introduced free economic zones. These favourable conditions need to be advertised to Indian business community to encourage the investment in Tajikistan.

Another area which has great potential of cooperation between India and Tajikistan is hydropower. Micro and mini hydroelectric power stations can be set up in remote areas of country with Indian help and experience in this field. Such involvement will take relations between the two countries to new level.[36]

Given the strategic importance of Tajikistan because of its location and the role which it can play for securing India's security interests in the region, New Delhi needs to intensify its existing defence and military cooperation. Some of the measures could be: annual security dialogue, active annual cooperation plan and cooperation in disaster management, and adventure sports. India can increase the number of seats for Tajik cadets in the National Defence Academy (NDA) and in National Defence College (NDC).

Some Indian observers are of the view that "India has to shed the current approach of understanding Central Asia steadfastly through Western prism" and it should "translate its 'soft power' into a strategic framework and make it linchpin of India's policy goal in Central Asia".[37] With respect to Tajikistan, India has already been involved in capacity building in many ways. However, the current initiatives can be further intensified in field of education, culture, science and technology, training in finance and banking sector and building much needed infrastructure in Tajikistan to re-harness and promote India's interests for long-term benefit.

Prognosis

Currently, South Asia—particularly, the Afghanistan-Pakistan region, Central Asian Region and West Asian region are getting exposed to a completely new set of security and economic challenges. The region is going through a major transition period. In the current context, no nation can address these new threats and challenges by itself and therefore the need for regional cooperation. Moreover, in the light of the U.S. withdrawal from Afghanistan in 2014, the regional countrics particularly India, Russia, China, Iran, Pakistan and CARs need to formulate and prepare long term policy options/solutions to address future challenges in the region. There is need for regional countries to work together for regional transportation networks and cooperation in energy sector for economic development, stability and peace in the region. While bilateral mechanism can continue, the regional cooperation should be encouraged because regional cooperation will not only bring economic prosperity in entire South-West and Central Asian region but also peace and stability. Arrangements based on balance of power are likely to deliver less than the arrangements based on collective peace. India and Tajikistan, close strategic partners can collectively play an important role in working along with other regional countries for creating mechanism of cooperation based on collective peace.

NOTES

1. Pakistan occupied Kashmir (PoK) is legally a part of the Indian State of Jammu & Kashmir as the former ruler of J&K signed the Instrument of Accession joining the Indian Union.

Tajikistan's border with China is 414 km, Uzbekistan 1,161 km, Kyrgyzstan 870 km and Afghanistan 1,206 km.

2. Views expressed by former Director IDSA, Jasjit Singh, in Rahul Bedi, "India dabbles in the new 'great game'," *Jane's Intelligence Review*, Vol.13 (6), June 2002, p.19.
3. B.R. Muthu Kumar, "India-Tajikistan Relations and the Quest for Regional Stability", K. Santhanam Ramakant Dwivedi (ed.) India-Tajikistan Cooperation Perspectives and Prospects, Delhi Anamaya Publishers, 2007, pp.23-25.
4. Ministry of External Affair Report (MEA), Government of India, 1993-94, p.28.
5. Ibid., 1995-96, p.33.
6. Opening Remark by Mahmadshoh Ilolov, President of Tajik Academy of Sciences, Dushanbe at the International Conference on "Geopolitical Dynamics of the Indo-Tajik Relations" 29 June 2010.
7. *Op.* cit., no. 4, 1997-98, p. 45 and 1998-99, pp. 34-35.
8. MEA Report, 2001-2002 p.34, and "India offers $5 m grant to Tajikistan", *Hindu*, May 11,2001.
9. Ibid., 2001-2002, pp.34-35.
10. http://www.dailyexcelsior.com/01may11/busi.htm
11. ITAR-TASS, News Agency, Moscow in English, 0937gmt January 30, 2003 in *BBC Monitoring Newsline,* January 31, 2003.
12. ITAR-TASS News Agency, Moscow, in English 1518gmt December 3, 2002.
13. Radio Free Europe/Radio Liberty (RFE/RL),Prague, Czech Republic, Central Asia Report, Vol.3(39), November 21, 2003.
14. http://mediandia.nic.in/speech/2006/08/04js01.htm; B.R. Mutu Kumar, "India-Tajikistan Relations: An Appraisal and Agenda for Future", Paper presented in International Seminar on "India and Tajikistan in International Affairs,"at Indian Council of World Affairs, New Delhi, August 8, 2006.
15. Joint Declaration by Republic of India and the Republic of Tajikstan on Further Development of Relations, Friendship and Cooperation, at http://meaindia.nic.in/declarestatement/2006/08/07jd01.htm
16. Information provided by Embassy of India in Dushanbe in June 2010 during authors visit.
17. Details about list of documents signed can be seen at (accessed on September 5, 2012)
18. Joint Statement on Strategic Partnership between the Republic of Tajikistan, September03,2012 at http://meaindia.nic.in/mystart.php?id=190019983 (accessed on September 4,2012)
19. Ibid.
20. India-Tajikistan Relations at http://meaindia.nic.in/mystart.php?id=50044531 (accessed on September 5, 2012)
21. Vidya Subrahmaniam, "Pratibha thanks Dushanbe for help to fight terror", *The Hindu*, Delhi, September, 8, 2010.
22. Ibid.
23. Ibid.
24. "A Perspective for Central Asia-India Relation: Common Ties of History", *The Times of Central Asia*, January 27, 2000. The Islamic geographer Yaqut noted in the twelfth century that "a prosperous merchant of Merve had one warehouse on the Volga river and another in Gujrat, India and he owned his prosperity to his role as a middle man in an exist of trade" Central Asia was a meeting point for traders and travellers, where mercantile communities lived in perfect harmony.

25. A. Mukhtarov, "Some Aspects of the History of Cultural Relations of Central Asia with India", Mahavir Singh, ed. India and Tajikistan Revitalising A traditional Relationship, Delhi, Anamika Publishers, 2003, pp.47-48. Mushtaq A. Kaw, "Indo-Tajik Relations: A historical Perspective", K Santhanam Ramakant Dwivedi (ed.) India-Tajikistan Cooperation Perspectives and Prospects, Delhi Anamaya Publishers, 2007, pp. 8-17.
26. At http://www.mea.gov.in/meaxpsite/foreignrelation/tajikistan.pdf (accessed on December 10,2010), Joint Statement on Strategic Partnership between the Republic of Tajikistan, September03,2012 at http://meaindia.nic.in/mystart.php?id=190019983 (accessed on September 4,2012), India-Tajikistan Relations at http://meaindia.nic.in/mystart.php?id=50044531 (accessed on September 5, 2012)
27. Views based on authors discussion during "III India Central Asia Regional Conference", 6-8 November 2003, Tashkent and also interaction by author during visits in 2008 (Tashkent), 2010 (Almaty and Bishkek) with scholars, officials, and other experts.
28. Colonel K.A. Muthanna, Enabling Military-to Military Cooperation As Foreign Policy Tool: Options for India, Knowledge World, New Delhi, 2006, pp. 135.
29. Ibid., pp. 135-36; Group of Ministers Report on Reforming the National Security System, New Delhi, Government of India, Feburary 2001.
30. RFE/RL Central Asia Report, 3 (39), November 21, 2003.
31. Rahul Bedi, "India dabbles in the new great game", *Jane's Intelligence Review,* Vol. 13(6), June 2002, p. 19.
32. The Military Balance, London, International Institute for Strategic Studies, p.170.
33. RFE/RL Central Asia Report, 3 (19), May 29, 2003.
34. Haji Umarov, "Tajik-Indian Economic Relations:Difficulties,Problems and Obstacles", Mahavir Singh, ed. India and Tajikistan Revitalising A traditional Relationship, Delhi, Anamika Publishers, 2003, p.104.
35. S. Dostboev, "Issues of cooperation of Tajikistan with India in the field of business and Technology" Mahivir Singh Ed. India and Tajikistan Revitalising a Traditional Relationship, Delhi, Animika Publishers & Distributors (P) Ltd. 2003, p.116.
36. A. Dilshot, "Strengthening India-Central Asia Cooperation: Especially Economic and Trade Relations", Paper Presented in India-Central Asia Seminar in New Delhi, September 11-12, 2000.
37. P. Stobdan, "India, Buddhism and Geopolitics in Central Asia: Regaining Centrality", IDSA Policy Brief, June 25, 2010.

8

Tajik-Indian Relations in the Mirror of Public Opinion in Tajikistan

Saodat Olimova and Muzaffar Olimov

The history of relations between the people of Tajikistan and India has its roots in deep antiquity. The whole territory of present day Tajikistan was a part of the Kushan Empire that joined Central Asia and India. Strong links have continued since the early 13th century in the era of the invasion of Muslims in India. Establishment and strengthening of the Mughal Empire in India (from 1526 till its disintegration in 18th century), gave additional impetus to relations, as the rulers maintained strong psychological and emotional ties with their homeland in Central Asia.

The warm relations between India and Central Asia were further developed in the Soviet era, when strong cooperation was established in the field of science, politics, economy and culture.

Thus, although India and Tajikistan enter in two different political-territorial regions, they have a common past, and the experience of interaction and mutual influence. Bearing in mind this common heritage, we set out to study how the people of Tajikistan now relate to India. The study attempted to find how citizens of Tajikistan assess various aspects of life in India—its political system, economy, international politics, culture and art. Other issues covered in this study included:

- What connects Tajikistan and India?
- What separates them?
- Whether the Tajiks consider India as an enemy, friend or partner?
- From what sources they get information about India and how they look at the prospects of Tajik-Indian relations.

Analysing the data of a public opinion survey conducted amongst 1,000 respondents in all cities of Tajikistan in June 2009, the study found that the Tajik society as a whole was friendly to India, but strongly felt that there was a great lack of information.

Table 1: Attitude Towards India

Indicator	*Frequency*	*Percent*
Very friendly	297	29.7
Rather friendly	640	64.0
Rather not friendly	53	5.3
Not very friendly	1	1
Do not know	8	8
Rejection	1	1
Total	1000	100.0

Twenty-nine percent of the respondents had a very favourable opinion about Indiawhile another 64 percent too were friendly. Only five percent of the respondents were unfriendly to India. If we compare the attitude towards India with other countries, firstly, we find that the Tajik's attitude to India is much better than that towards China and EU countries, but significantly less than Russia and Iran. This suggests that India has the sympathy of citizens of Tajikistan, but this sympathy did not reach the level of Iran, which in Tajik society is considered as a cultural metropolis, and Russia, the undisputed leader and patron in the eyes of public opinion in Tajikistan.

A high population of Tajikistan appreciates the culture of India, its music, and, above all, Indian films—almost 38 percent reported that they admire Indian films, 19 percent admire Indian music, and 17 percent highly appreciated India's culture.

Regarding international politics of India as a matter of respect for the people of Tajikistan—every 10th respondent highly appreciated India's policy in the international arena. Less enthusiastic citizens of Tajikistan think about the national (domestic) policy of India—it is supported by about eight per cent of respondents. A small number of respondents—three percent admire the economic system of India and its religious policy.

The least sympathy is towards the India political system (two per cent)—because of the very large differences with the Tajik political system.

Table 2: The Reason for a Favourable Attitude to India

Indicator	*Frequency*	*Valid Percent*
I appreciate its economic system	30	3.2
I appreciate its political system	23	2.5
I appreciate the religious policy of India	30	3.2
I appreciate the international policy of India	92	9.8
I appreciate the national policy of India	72	7.7
I admire its culture	156	16.6
I admire her music	180	19.2
I admire the Indian movies	353	37.7
I do not know	1	1
Total	937	100.0

Although only a very small percentage of the interviewees did not have a friendly view of India, deeper inquiry revealed that there were three issues of negativism. Particularly, tense relations with Pakistan which threatened the stability of the whole region. About half of those who had a malevolent attitude to India cited this as a cause. Equally important is the contradiction between Hindus and Muslims in India. The third problem that causes negativity towards India, is India's position in relation to the Kashmir issue. However, we should not forget that only five per cent of the respondents had a malevolent attitude to India and all three of these problems wee related to Islam. This is not surprising, bearing in mind the rapid revival of Islam in the post-Soviet Tajikistan.

Table 3: Reason for Unfavourable Attitude Towards India

Indicators	*Frequency*	*Valid Percent*
I do not like conflict with Pakistan	26	48.1
India's position on Kashmir issue	12	22.2
Relation to Islam	16	29.6
Total	54	100,0

The study specifically examined public opinion in Tajikistan on attitudes to India and Islam and found only slightly more than six percent of respondents believed that India is against Muslims, 83 percent do not believe in this, and 10 percent do not know about it. During cross-analysis, the study revealed that people who believed that India wass against the Muslims—were active Muslims following the world policy and were informed about the religious controversy in South Asia. They are ill-disposed towards India because of the Indo-Pakistani conflict, Kashmir issue and Indo-Muslim communalism. Others have little or no knowledge about these issues, but are confident that India, with its high culture and traditions of nonviolence will not infringe upon the rights of Muslims.

Table 4: Is India Against Muslims?

Indicators	*Frequency*	*Percent*
Strongly agree	15	1.5
Rather, I agree	49	4.9
Rather, do not agree	326	32,6
Totally disagree	507	50.7
Do not know	100	10,0
Rejection	3	3
Total	1000	100.0

Talking about the attitude of the Tajikistan people to India, it should be noted that India is not in the list of countries, representing a potential threat to Tajikistan, i.e. its enemies. About half of respondents believe that Tajikistan in general has no enemies. Others believe that the potential threat could be from neighbouring Uzbekistan and Afghanistan. In this list are USA and Russia, China and European countries, and Pakistan, but India is not, which means, that no one in Tajikistan considers India as a country, carrying a potential threat.

On the question of where Tajik society receives information about India. The study found that the main source of information about India is the national television. About 38 percent of respondents know about India from national television. 14 percent learn about India from the stories of relatives and friends. Other sources like, radio, local and international television, and newspapers are the only source of information for every tenth respondent.

Table 5: Primary Source of Information about India

Indicators	*Frequency*	*Valid Percent*
Local/regional television	101	10.2
National television	373	37.7
International television	104	10.5
Newspapers	93	9.4
Radio	112	11.3
Magazines	24	2.4
Internet	17	1.7
Relatives and friends	133	13.4
Do not know	33	3.3
Total	990	100.0

We were interested in public opinion on the prospects of Tajik-Indian relations. We found that 76 percent were satisfied with the development of Tajik-Indian relations, but they believed that they could be even better. Seventeen percent believe it was necessary to fully develop its relations with India, considering it as a very important potential partner. Only two percent believe that relations with India must be frozen. This two percent again come from a group of Islamists who are unhappy with attitude towards Islam in India.

Table 6: Tajik-India Relations

Indicators	*Frequency*	*Percent*
Yes, the Tajik-Indian relations are satisfactory	374	37.4
Yes, but they could be better	378	37.8
No, we must develop relations with India	172	17.2
No, we must reduce relations with India	25	2.5
Other	1	1
Do not know	50	5.0
Total	1000	100.0

Findings

1. The history of relations between the Tajiks and the Indians is long. Ties between thc two have been stableand the diversity of cultural contacts provides an extremely friendly attitude of the population of Tajikistan to India.
2. The population of Tajikistan appreciates the art and culture of India which they are familiar with and have historically highly valued.
3. There are stumbling blocks in the development of Tajik-Indian relations: Firstly, a profound difference in political cultures, and secondly, a very low level of economic relations, because of which the public opinion has a low estimate of India's economy. Thirdly, and mainly, is the issue of Islam, which concerns the Indo-Pakistan conflict, Kashmir problem and the Hindu-Muslim communalism. However, only a small percentage of population in Tajikistan has a negative view of India on this score.
4. Overall the public opinion of Tajikistan regards India as an ally and friend. None of the respondents named India as a potential enemy.
5. There is a scarcity of sources of information about India. The

greatest amount of information about India is provided by the state television, which reflects the policy of the Republic of Tajikistan for the maintenance of the Tajik-Indian relations.

6. According to public opinion the level of the Tajik-Indian relations is satisfactory, but has potential for development. A fifth of the respondents believe that the Tajik-Indian relations should be fully developed and that it would be beneficial to Tajikistan.

9
Literature brings People Together

Habibullo Rajabob

The role of literature in shaping relations between nations is enormous. True literature largely brings people and cultures closer. Newspaper and magazine articles as well as other information—no matter what they are—even slogans and appeals to friendly relations and cooperation cannot exist for a long time and win the love and affection of people for many centuries. But a literary work lives a long life and when the same is translated into other languages, it contributes to the convergence of different peoples speaking different languages.

These were the early postwar years. More precisely, it was in March of 1947, when famous Tajik poet, Mirzo Tursunzade, first visited India as a member of the Soviet delegation. It was just before the attainment of India's independence. The poet returned from India with a tremendous impression. His feelings were expressed in 13 poems that were published under the title 'The Indian Ballad'. This collection of poems includes such verses as 'The Return', 'Indian Ballad', 'Western Guest', 'Tara Chandra', 'Taj Mahal', 'Hanging Garden', 'The River Ganga', 'My Toast', 'Traveller of India', 'Raised in Memory', 'The Hat of Professor Akhvlediani', 'In the Dream of the Nest' and 'Two Roads'. After these verses were published, the popularity of poet Mirzo

Tursunzade grew even further. The poems were the fruits of reflection of the poet-humanist, an indefatigable fighter for peace and cooperation among nations.

Within a short time they were translated into Russian, English, Portuguese, Spanish, Polish, Chinese, Hindi, Georgian, Uzbek, Kazakh and other languages of the world and the Soviet Union.

Thus, thanks to these verses, before the—readers—speaking in different languages and representing diverse countries and cultures—opened up a panorama of Indian life as seen by the great poet during his short stay in this beautiful country. Thanks to the 'Indian Ballad', the popularity of the Tajik poet rapidly spread in the whole world, but most importantly, in India. India's remarkably talented people and great art became even closer and dearer for the Tajik people. Although already in the 1920s Tajik poets addressed the Indian theme, but only the mighty pen of Mirzo Tursunzade could give to both the simple as well as the highly educated Tajik readers of the time, what they wanted to know about India.

In addition to the reflection of the Indian theme in the works of Tajik poets andwriters, mention may also be made of the translation and publication of Indian literature in the Tajik language and the translation of the works of Tajik writers in Indian languages. Fiction is always the most important source of knowledge of a country. Tajikistan began to actively translate the works of Indian authors since the fifties of last century. It should be noted that at that time translations were done only through the Russian language, as Tajikistan did not still have local interpreters who knew the Indian languages, so that they could directly translate from the original work. Thus, the Russian language acted as a mediator between Indian languages and Tajik language. In such a situation such interpreters were needed who could convey artistic images, thoughts, ideas and other features of the literary work with maximum precision and clarity. Keeping in view the growing interest of their countrymen in India and its rich multicultural literature, such highly qualified Tajik translators as Sharif Sharaf, Mullokandov N., Abdujalil Vositzoda, Hasan Irfon, Rahim Hoshim, Pulod Tolis, Hikmat Rahmat and others, translated from

Russian to Tajik language more than 300 short stories, narratives, novels, fables and poems by Indian authors within a span of only 30 years from 1950 to 1980. Undoubtedly, the best works of talented and well-known masters of artistic expression were translated in the Russian language in the first place and then the creation of young and, of course, promising poets and writers of India. Tajik translators also maintained this tradition and from the rich repository had the opportunity to select the best of the best. In addition, the criteria for selection were—and of course, continue to be so today also—the artistic value and humanistic orientation of a particular product.

During the decades of the fifties and sixties, most of the translations included the works of Rabindranath Tagore, Premchand, Mohan Singh and Khwaja Ahmad Abbas. Among the above-mentioned authors particularly popular in Tajikistan were the works of Rabindranath Tagore and Premchand and this remains so to this day. Tagore during his life time enjoyed incredible popularity both in his homeland and abroad. In 1961, the birth centenary of Rabindranath Tagore was widely observed around the world, including in Tajikistan. Tagore, the great Indian poet, writer, thinker, artist and the first Nobel Prize winner from the entire East, was already well known in our country. In 1940 the Tajik language journal 'By Lenin's Way' published Tagore's story 'One Lucky Night'. Subsequently his other works were translated. In 1958, Hasan Irfon translated the novel 'The Wreck'. The publication of the works of Indian authors and especially those of Rabindranath Tagore in Tajikistan, is an important event. This is another proof of the successful development of cultural relations between the two countries and serves as a prime example of mutual understanding of peoples of India and Tajikistan.

The year 1961 in Tajikistan could be regarded as the year of Rabindranath Tagore. For nearly a year works of Tagore and articles about him were published. That was the year when the Tajik readers in their native language were acquainted with such stories of the writer as 'Kabuliwalla', 'Mahamaya', 'Notebook', 'Renunciation', 'Suspicion', etc. But the biggest event in the cultural life of Tajikistan was the translation of Tagore's famous novel 'Gora', where the reader is primarily acquainted with the spiritual life of Indian society during the colonial period. Tagore's play 'The Sacrifice' was also translated and published in Tajik language. In the same year, the Tajik readers with great interest were acquainted with excerpts from the famous poetry collection of the poet 'The Gardener'. Tagore in his short stories and novels depicts everyday life and experiences of Hindus, reveals a panorama of the spiritual life of the people of India in the late 19th and early 20th century. Later, another novel by Tagore 'A Grain of Sand' translated by Sharafjan Pulatova in Tajik language was published. This translation was also done from Russian language.

It was only in 2006 that for the first time 19 stories of Tagore were translated from Hindi to Tajik. Published under the general title 'Selected Stories', they included, 'The Judge', 'One Night', 'Dahlia', 'Hemanti', 'Farewell Night', 'Elder Sister', 'Stranger', 'Punishment' and others. They were translated by me together with my other colleagues—teachers of the Department of Indian Philology, Tajik National University (TNU)—M. Usmanov, Z. Rakhmatullaeva, M. Solieva and Z. Afsakhova. The presentation of this collection was held both in Dushanbe as well as Delhi. On August 7, 2006 during the state visit of President Emomali Rahmon to India the book was released in Delhi. President Rahmon and Minister of State for External Affairs of India Mr. Ahmad personally witnessed the presentation of the book. This was another proof of the huge respect for the Indian genius.

Reading the works of Rabindranath Tagore, we learn many valuable and interesting things about India, about her hard-working and peaceful people, and become imbued with great respect for everything that relates to this wonderful country. Once we have got to know in greater detail the works of Tagore and also how India gained Independence, it seems to us that India is not so far away. Now we want to know more about independent India, about how she decides her fate and what gave her freedom. Any information in this regard was interesting, but fiction, created by realist writers—as already mentioned—gave what no other source could provide.

Along with Tagore, more and more interest is growing in wider Indian literature that has a long history of 4,000 years. Research and publication by the Tajik scholars of a number of scientific—research works on India in the field of literature, language, history and art have further contributed to the growing interest in Indian literature.

In the seventies and eighties translated in the Tajik language were works of Vishnu Prabhakar, Balkrishna, Krishan Chandar, Dhani Ram Chatrik, Harindranatha Chattopadhyaya, Yashpal, Agyeya, Upendranath Ashk, Vallathol, Gopichanda, Gurcharan Rampur, Kartar Singh Duggal, Premchand, Amrita Pritam, Gurbakhsh Singh, Mohan Singh, Bankimchandra Chattopadhyaya, Subhadra Kumari Chauhan and others.

Since Tajikistan gained independence, a new era of cultural cooperation between the peoples of India and Tajikistan has begun. This, of course, is the topic of much larger discussion. It is with this historical event that qualitatively new avenues of research and translation of Indian literature are linked. At the beginning of the new millennium in 2002, a collection of stories of contemporary writers in India was published in the Tajik language. It includes 18 stories of 14 well-known writers, mostly writers in Hindi. Some of these writers, such as Premchand, Yashpal, Upendranath Ashk and Krishan Chandra have long been familiar to the Tajik readers, but the stories of Madhavrao Sapre, Uday Prakash, Munimankiyam Narasimha Rao, Mohan Rakesh, Mannu Bhandari and others were offered for the first time. It was the first attempt to translate the stories of Indian writers directly from the original language.

In 2003, in honour of the official visit of the Prime Minister of India, Mr. Atal Bihari Vajpayee to Tajikistan, I translated his collection of poems 'A drop of rain' from Hindi to Tajik. With this collection, we learned that Mr. Vajpayee is not only a prominent political figure, but also a wonderful poet.

The publication of this book was another foundation stone for the building of the Tajik-Indian friendship. In 2007, a collection of translations by famous Tajik interpreter Hikmat Rahmat entitled 'Voices of Friends' was published in two volumes. All translations were made from Russian language. In this beautiful bouquet 28 poems of six prominent Indian poets such as Bhai Vir Singh, Dhaniram Chatrik,

Mohan Singh, Gurcharan Rampur, Amrita Pritam and Subhadra Kumari Chauhan found a worthy place. A year later, also in the translation from Russian to Tajik, was published a collection of stories by Indian writers, entitled 'Gift of India'. Translator and author of the preface is Sharafbonu Pulatova. It includes 14 stories of eight writers of different literatures of India.

Mohan Rakesh was a talented novelist and playwright of India. In 2007, my translation of his collection of short stories 'The Sad Life' was published. In 2009 a monograph on Phanishvarnath Renu was published. In this book the translation of two stories of Renu was done based on the model of the creative manner of the writer, including the story 'The third oath', which entered into the golden fund of the Indian and world literature. This story introduces us to the life and customs of ordinary people of northern India.

About translations of Tajik authors in Indian language—Indian readers have been familiar with the works of prominent Tajik writer Sadriddin Aini for more than 60 years. This was thanks to famous Indian writer, scientist, translator and traveller Rahul Sankrityayan (1893-1963), who in the forties of the last century began a serious study of literature and the history of the peoples of Central Asia. He was particularly interested in modern Tajik literature. After reading the works of Sadriddin Aini, Mirzo Tursunzade, Jalol Ikrami, Sotim Ulugzade and Rahim Jalil, he began to translate the work of Sadriddin Aini, and in 1948 two of his translated works were published in Hindi, namely: The story 'Odina' and the novel 'Dokhunda'. The preface is written by translator to both books and an afterword to the novel 'Dokhunda'. Notably, Rahul Sankrityayan thinks Sadriddin Aini is Premchand of Central Asia, and adds:

> "Novels of Aini 'Dokhunda' and 'Slave' are not only artistic but also historical works. Of course, there are many sources and methods to get acquainted with Central Asia since the Soviet Union, however, it may be said without any exaggeration that the works of Sadriddin Aini are most suitable for this purpose."

The same idea is also expressed by the publisher of the book.

In 1952, Rahul Sankrityayan translated into Hindi, the most popular book of Aini 'The Death of the Usurer', and in 1953—the novel 'Slaves'. Three years later he translated the novel 'The Orphan'. Thus, Rahul Sankrityayan translated into Hindi nearly all the known works of the Tajik writer. Later these works have been repeatedly reprinted in different cities of India. The translator explained the reasons for the popularity of the Tajik writer in the preface to the novel 'The Death of the Usurer', where, he particularly emphasises that the main cause of such interest is the desire to know more about the life of the people of the neighboring state.

Our narrative about the importance of literature in bringing people together, should have begun with highlighting how popular in our country are the works of Amir Khusrau Dehlavi, Bedil, Zebunisso and other great Persian poets of India. However, this is such a vast subject and in this respect so much work has been done that it deserves to be the subject of a separate speech.

Thus, despite all the innovations in the field of convergence of various people, literature, in our opinion, as before, remains the most reliable means of understanding and mutual enrichment between nations.

10

Some Problems of Research of Persian Literature of India

Sh. Sufiev

First and foremost let me express my gratitude to organisers of this conference—the President of Tajik Academy of sciences Mr. Mahmadshoh Ilolov and Mr. Sudhir Devare, the Director General of Indian Council of World Affairs and His Excellency the Ambassador of India to Tajikistan Mr. Amar Sinha for organising this conference and greetings to all the participants and guests from India who have gathered here.

On behalf of the Institute of Oriental studies of Tajikistan's Academy of Sciences, I would like to express our most sincere consideration to India and its Embassy in Dushanbe for the considerable efforts that they are making to strengthen and develop India-Tajikistan Bilateral cooperation during the last 18 years.

It is known, that without knowledge of the past it is impossible to understand the present. These words are especially true, when it concerns the relations of our two people in the past and the present. Studying of these relations will open up much in common between our two people who earlier had a common Indo-Iranian identity I shall not dwell on relations of the people of India and Tajikistan throughout history. I wish to just highlight in brief the very important and valuable page of the richest history of India which for us, Tajiks, has huge value.

Since the epoch of extreme antiquity, close historical and cultural contacts connected India and the Central Asia—these two original centres of culture of the East. Researches of Tajik archeologists Ranov, Litwinski, Mandelshtam, Pugacheko and others show typological affinity of cultures of Tajikistan and India in the epochs of Paleolithic, Neolithic, Achaemenids and the Kushans. Many archeological items of these periods found in Ajina-Teppe, Varash, Penjikent and Afrasiab, now decorate our National museum and other museums of Tajikistan. They personally speak of our very close cultural contacts with India.

This unity of our people, has also been fixed on the pages *of Rigveda* and *Avesta*—the general pantheon of Gods and many rituals and traditions imprinted in these two monumental works. They tell us about the common reflections of Indo-Aryan people about the nature and the world, about system of cosmogony ideas and rudiments of philosophical knowledge. This basic, fundamental knowledge helped so that subsequently in the Middle Ages there were powerful processes of cultural and intellectual exchange. The later Vedic literature –the epic poems 'Ramayana' and 'Mahabharata' were translated in Persian language. These texts were not foreign for Iranian people as that uniform generality which was emphasised above, formed uniform tastes and sights.

We consider that powerful development of intellectual life during the Muslim period of history of the Indian subcontinent was also based on this unity. In fact during the period of Great Mughals' rule in India such huge quantity of scientific, literary and historical monuments were created, which exceeded by quantity the literary work created in all other Iranian areas. Therefore, Herman Ette fairly names this period of history of the Persian literature as 'the Indian summer of the Persian literature'.

The degree of the level of scrutiny of any historical period appreciably depends on sources which the researcher has. As far as we know, the enormous quantity of the most unique literary and religious-philosophical writings in the Persian language which were created in days of the Muslim period in India is kept in book-depositories and libraries of India. This layer of the Indian culture for us Tajiks is very valuable to us in the same way as to the local Indian people, as our ancestors also took active part in the creation of that heritage. Moreover, the aesthetic and literary style that developed in the Indian subcontinent known as 'The Indian Style' of Persian literature was until the first two decades of the 20th century the basic style in our area.

For us it is important to keep today the traditions of research on Indo-Persian literature of India in Tajikistan, begun by Ustad Aini, B. Gafurov and A. Mirzoev.

Owing to independence of Tajikistan we in Dushanbe now have an Embassy of India which provides a lot of works in all the spheres of a life of our society. For Tajiks, India has turned from the fantastic, inaccessible country to the friendly country which any interested person can visit. But, alas, social scientists, engaged in researching the history of Indo-Persian philosophy and literature, do not have many such opportunities. It would be the great contribution of the Indian state to facilitate the study of the intellectual life of the Indian subcontinent during the Great Mughals and to provide all-necessary help to Our Academy of Sciences in the development of researches in this direction: to create conditions for visiting India and working in the richest libraries of India in which the great variety of the written heritage are preserved that have not still entered in a scientific turnover and to create the special Centre of the Indo-Tajik researches to bring together the best specialists from our two countries.

All this in reality will strengthen the roots of that mighty tree of unity and friendship which remains alive till now despite all historical hardships and sorrows and continues to give fruits which we hope will continue to fructify till life on the Earth remains.

11

Cultural Relations between Tajikistan, Iran and the Indian Connection

Mirzo Mulloahmedov

Tajik-Iranian cultural relations have a very ancient history. The relationship of these peoples is related primarily to their commonality in ethnic origin, common language, customs, religion, culture, etc.

As is known, for thousands of years these people have created a single world-famous culture. Only in the 16th century, after the establishment of the Safavid state in Iran and Sheibanid in Maverannahr various curtains and borders were drawn between these two kindred nations.

Although for more than five centuries, political, economic and cultural processes in these countries were separated from each other, but the cultural relations between the Tajik and Iranian people could never cease. These relations were carried on primarily through trade caravans on the Silk Road.

During the Soviet times there were no direct relations between Tajikistan and Iran. All relations were conducted through Moscow. However, the cultural relations between the Tajik and Iranian people continued. For example, in 20th century, in Tajikistan the collections of works of such prominent writers and poets of Iran such as M. Bahar, Iraj Mirza, Dehkhuda, Saeed Nafisi, S. Kasrai, Sadeq Hedayat, Buzurg Alavi, Furugh Farrukhzad, Nadir Nadirpur, Jawad Fazil, etc were published. In Iran were published 'Memoirs of S. Aini', 'Feruza' of Jalal Ikrami, works of M. Tursunzade, S. Ulughzade, Ubaid Rajab, M. Hakimova, A. Dehoti, B. Rahimzade, A. Shukuhi, etc.

The founder of modern Tajik literature S. Aini played a great role in rebuilding the cultural ties between the Tajik and Iranian peoples. In his articles he presented the Tajik people to the events that occurred in Iran in the early 20th century.

In the expansion of cultural relations between the two peoples, Lahuti played an especially important role. He is considered as an Iranian as well as a Tajik poet. After moving to the USSR, he chose Tajikistan as his second home and made an enormous contribution to the development of modern literature and culture of the Tajik people.

M. Tursunzade also greatly contributed in strengthening the Tajik-Iranian cultural relations. By his initiative in 1968 the International Symposium of poetry of Persian-speaking peoples was organised in Dushanbe. The symposium was attended by well-known Iranian poets and literary figures like, Parviz Natel Khanlari, Lutfali Suratgar and Nadir Nadirpur.

The symposium was truly a festival of friendship of Persian-speaking people.

Iranian scientists S. Nafisi and Parviz Natel Khanlari also contributed greatly in strengthening the cultural relations between the two peoples in the 20th century.

Iranian scientists S. Nafisi, Parviz Natel Khanlari, B. Furuzonfar, Farooqi, A. Zarinkub, B. Atabay participated in international scientific conferences devoted to 550th anniversary of Jami (1964), 650th anniversary of Hafiz (1971), 700th anniversary of Amir Khusrau Dehlavi (1975). Amir Khusrau hailed from India.

The collapse of the Soviet Union and the acquisition of national independence of Tajikistan opened a new stage in the development of Tajik-Iranian relations in all spheres of life. Consideration of all spheres of this cooperation requires a lot of time. Therefore, we briefly point out only some of the main events of the Tajik-Iranian relations in the cultural sphere.

The Iranian Embassy in Tajikistan and its cultural representation provided full cooperation to the development of cultural relations between Tajikistan and Iran. Multiple visits to Iran by Tajik artists, musicians, filmmakers, and other representatives of the Tajik art have been organised from time-to-time.

In the cities of Dushanbe and Khujand exhibitions of books, technology research and cultural centres in Iran were organised. Several times festivals of Iranian films were held in the cities of Tajikistan.

In the first years of independence in Dushanbe bookstores of Iranian publishers 'Surush' and 'Alhuda' were opened.

A notable cultural event was the establishment of a library of Rudaki in the building of the Republican Library of Firdausi. The opening ceremony of the library, which contains more than 14,000 books, was attended by the then Iranian Foreign Minister Aliakbar Vilayati. These libraries were also organised in Khujand, Penjikent, Kulyab and other cities of the republic.

Iran began to pay more attention to modern culture of Tajik people. In publishing houses and periodical press of Iran works of Tajik poets, writers and scientists were published. Only at the initiative of a connoisseur and scholar of modern Tajik literature, foreign member of Academy of Sciences (AS) of Republic of Tajikistan, the ambassador of Islamic Republic of Iran in Tajikistan Professor Aliasghar Sherdust various publishing houses of Iran have issued more than 120 works of Tajik writers, poets and scholars, including collections of works of M. Kanoat, Loik, Gulrukhsor, Gulnazar, Farzona, Askar Hakim, Ashur Safar, Kamol Nasrullah, Mehmon Bakhti, A. Samadov, M. Shakouri, M. Ajami, M. Shukurzade etc.

Tajik scientists M. Shakouri, and A. Maniyazov became members of the Academy of Language and Literature in Iran. A number of Tajik writers and scientists have received various awards of Islamic Republic of Iran (IRI).

Many Tajik and Iranian scientists have close scientific contacts. They organise joint scientific conferences, seminars, symposia.

Currently, under the leadership of Tajik scientists more than 500 Iranian graduate students and candidates' doctoral dissertations are prepared in Tajikistan.

Despite great strides, there are a lot of unresolved issues in the Tajik-Iranian cultural relations. For example, despite the interest in the country, it has still not created any joint middle and high school. Joint publishing and printing houses have not been set up. Institution of joint television of three Persian-speaking countries (Iran, Afghanistan, Tajikistan), has been delayed, although an agreement was signed on this long time ago.

Cooperation in the field of cinematography is very weak. Almost all the periodical press of Iran has been completely terminated in Tajikistan.

On this occasion it is appropriate to raise the issue of Indian scientists. As it is known, the large museums and libraries of India have tens of thousands of manuscripts in Persian. However, they are not studied, but even their catalogues are not made. It is time to create a joint tripartite Research Centre for the study of data of manuscripts, many of which are on the brink of destruction.

Many scientific and cultural institutions of our republic are using the existing opportunities and potentials in the Tajik-Iranian cultural relations insufficiently. Using these features certainly may contribute to the further expansion of Tajik-Iranian and Indian relations and the development of culture in the region and worldwide.

Index